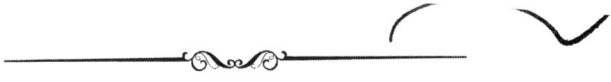

MW01526868

Joyful Living

Your Guide to Purpose and Passion

by

Dr. Neslyn Watson-Druée, CBE

Limited Edition Printed March 2016

Reprinted April 2016

Published by Createspace

Table of Contents

About The Author

— Dr Neslyn Watson-Druée CBE, FRCN, FCGI

International Speaker, Business Psychologist and CEO of Neslyn.com and Beacon Organisational Development. She is an inaugural awardee of 100 Best Global Coaching Leaders by the World HRD Congress. Dr Neslyn's unique business system *Beacon's Leadership Star System*™ and its sub-system *The Leader's Code*™ is used worldwide to change organisational culture, develop creativity, and care about people. Her other books include Fly High-Land Safely: The Definitive Book on Career Transition for Executives; The Beacon Leadership Technique—6 Conscious Blueprints to Experience Your Joy—A Guide to Relationships for Executives; The Beacon Technique: Leadership from Impossible to Possible and Authentic Choice: Be You.

Dr Neslyn has presented to the European Parliament, public and private sector organisations and various charities on the topics of leadership development, leaving a legacy, living with purpose and passion.

Dr Neslyn has received three separate awards form Her Majesty Queen Elizabeth II, including Commander of the British Empire and Queen Elizabeth II Medal. She is a certified High Performance Coach, Thinking Environment® coach and consultant and One Command® coach with expertise in emotional intelligence, creating and sustaining high performing teams. Dr Neslyn enables her clients to access their greater capacity that allows them to step into their greatness. She has 20+ years Board Level experience. She has a number of awards. Among them the National Training Award UK, Consultancy and Training Award, British Diversity Award, Diversity Persuader of the Decade, Author's Award from Radio Works World, The Millennium Nurse—Special Recognition Award, Fellowship of the Royal College of Nursing, Fellowship of the City and Guilds London Institute and Doctor of the University—Bradford and Birmingham City University.

Dr Neslyn is the host of Radio Works World Passion Show.

About Joyful Living

Do you leap out of bed each morning in joyful anticipation of the day? Are you proud of the legacy you are leaving with each word you speak and each action you take?

If so, then you are among the lucky 1% of people who know why they are here on Earth and are living in line with that knowledge. If you are like most of us however, you suspect that there must be something more to life than just surviving from day to day, even if you are "doing well" in a material sense.

Perhaps you have attained the outer markers of success, but you still have the nagging feeling that something is missing from your life. You know deep down that there is a big difference between living a joyful life spent doing what you love and just getting by with 'good enough', but you may be overwhelmed at what you believe it will take to get from good to great.

In this book I share what I have learned about how to find your life's passion and purpose, and how to use that knowledge to create a life of joy. I know that such a life can be yours—in fact, it is your birth-right to claim right now! Find the help in these pages to be whole, strong, joyful and passionate. In Joyful Living: Your Guide to Purpose and Passion, you will find practical wisdom, advice and actionable steps to help you get there, one step at a time.

— Dr Neslyn Watson-Druée, CBE

Foreword

The room was packed with people and some were standing, and for a moment I thought that must be the torrential rain outside that brought them all in at the same time. As I finished sharing my story, I left the stage, to be hugged by so many people, coming towards me with generous smiles and startling eyes; the space was filled with great, positive energy and I could hardly remember all the names I had to autograph my book to ...

The whole experience was a bit surreal, as I never thought my book could be that good... and, it wasn't the book, it was my story they loved, more than the book... And then, an elegant lady, wearing a turquoise dress came along with a beautiful smile, introduced herself and said: " We will do great works together" and she left.

Never been too good at collecting people's details or remembering their names, but that sentence stayed with me for a long time... For just over a thousand days actually, when we've met again!

Imagine the pure Joy I felt recognising the lady with the turquoise dress, who sat at the Round Table, helping us to celebrate the radio presenters and story tellers who won the Radio W.O.R.K.S. World Awards 2016. Since, we created and delivered great W.O.R.K.S. together, exactly as she said a thousand day ago!

If the language that children create with the purity of their imagination is the definition of joy, this is what Neslyn Watson-Druée's genius is bringing in my life: Pure Joy! Neslyn Watson-Druée is not only a gift to your life, but to humanity! Her Majesty, our divine Monarch, thinks the world of Neslyn to have honoured Neslyn three times, so, do I think the world of Neslyn!

In complete spiritual alignment, Neslyn is not only a very accomplished Author but the river of love, light, peace, compassion and harmony. The power for good in the world, a presence of all humanity and radiant energy, Neslyn teaches you to be plenty, enough and fun. She is determined to make a difference and leave a positive legacy in the world, and, yes, she does. Reading Neslyn's book, and her twelve books are just the beginning of her legacy, is a blissful experience and in reality, your reality, Neslyn helps you, the reader to unlearn what you knew about yourself and the world at large, to feel upbeat and confident, to wake up to a new reality: YOUR JOYFULL SELF.

Below are just a few of the nuggets you will gain from these pages:

- Why joy and success are your birth right
- How you can follow your passion to discover your purpose
- How to change your limiting beliefs so you can choose your thoughts
- Why no one else can tell you your truth, and how to learn to hear the wisdom of your heart

If you can open your mind, you will receive from Joyful Living: Your Guide to Purpose and Passion many treasures for your journey to a life of joy, passion and purpose.

— Marina Nani

Founder of the Academy of Significance™, Radio W.O.R.K.S. World and The Hotel Alternative. Author of the best-selling Away From Home and The Simple Truth book series

Introduction

We all want the fulfilment and happiness that comes with a life lived in accordance with who we are here to be, giving the gifts that only we can give. Yet many of us struggle to hone in on what living 'on purpose' looks like in our day-to-day lives. I am here to tell you that it is possible to not only find your purpose, but to live it. In this book I share what I have learned about living a purposeful life knowing that it can help you get there just as it has helped my clients over the years. I will also share what I have learned about the relationship between purpose and passion, which can be described as the feeling you have when you are living from your purpose. If you feel you do not know your purpose, then it is your passion that can lead you there.

Ch. 1: Arriving at a Life of Purpose

The book begins with my personal story of how I arrived at a life centred on Passion and Purpose, and my experiences helping my clients to do the same. There is an illuminating section on Intention and Attention and how reality is created from where you put your attention, both within and without.

Ch. 2: Joy is Your Birth Right

This chapter focuses on the relationship between joy, purpose and passion. What are the signs and symptoms of a life not lived on purpose, and how do you find the possibility for something different? The secret to living on purpose is to find a way to serve the highest good of both yourself and others. Purpose is about committing to be living your highest and best good in service (passion). How do you fulfil your purpose, both inner and outer?

There are clarifying questions to enable you on your Journey to your Purpose:

'If I were absolutely committed to living my highest and best good, how would I be? What would I do?"

The universe will always give you your highest commitment. But you will need to take a chance on faith.

There is an exercise to clarify: What do you see in the overall pattern of your life? Where you are now reflects every choice you have made up to this point. You are the only person whose permission you need to thrive, and you learn how to give it to yourself by embracing where you are right now. You need to start, so you can arrive.

Ch. 3: Where Passion and Purpose Meet

Many people experience their inner purpose as being the fount from which their outer purpose springs, and this makes sense when you consider that to align with our inner purpose means to align with the Divine within you. When you are thus connected, you know exactly what to do and when to do it, and it doesn't matter to you whether you know how to do it or not because you know that God has willed it to happen through you. A true experience of purpose is an experience of faith, faith in yourself and the One who made you. What could you accomplish if you know you could not fail, and that you were loved no matter what?

Ch. 4: Let Go of What Keeps You From Living With Joy, Purpose and Passion

I provide tools to help you create yourself anew each day. Among them is the need to fully accept yourself and to believe that you already have what it takes to reach your goals.

Within the chapter there is a discussion on the perils of limiting beliefs – specifically, how they can prevent you from actualizing or even knowing your purpose. For example, the belief that you are unworthy of living a life of purpose and fulfilment, or that service to others requires you to sacrifice yourself. These are deep-seated beliefs that can be very difficult to release on your own. While the perspective of a trusted friend or family member can be helpful, we aren't all blessed with good relationships with people we have known most of our lives. In this case, a trained coach can help you uncover the meaning that your life's patterns reveal, not telling you the answer but helping you reach it in much less time than you could on your own. This is where my break-though coaching and One Command™ Approach is invaluable.

Ch. 5: Place Your Purpose at the Centre of Your Life

This chapter explores how to integrate what you have learned into the daily rhythms of your life.

Within the chapter, there is extensive discussion of the journey made by Anita Moorjani, author of Dying to Be Me and What If This is Heaven, whose commitment to being her authentic self after her near-death experience totally changed her life. While hers is an extraordinary story, it reinforces the idea that anything is possible when you fully align with your true self.

To get started on the new, you must first shed what no longer works. That is not always the easiest thing to do. However, when you understand that the key to success lies mainly in having the courage to be who you are, magic happens.

Ch. 6: Commit to Your Purpose Now

This chapter explores why it is important to live life on your own terms. It looks at Bronnie Ware's book The Top Five Regrets of The Dying to underline why it is important to spend your life doing what matters. Why stand in the way of your own happiness, especially when happiness is a choice? Can today be the day you change your life? Of course it can!

The old narrative of 'power over' calls us to out-smart and out-compete others, with their 'surrender' as the hallmark of our victory. This patriarchal model of power is still all too prevalent in human organisations, but for some years now we have seen more inclusive, collaborative leadership models begin to take hold.

What does this have to do with the kind of surrender I am talking about, and what does it have to do with purpose? How many times have you quashed your truth out of fear that others would react negatively, or even denied it to yourself because of your limiting beliefs?

Surrendering to the greatness that the Universe has planned for you takes courage, but it is also one of the fastest ways to arrive at a life lived on purpose. All you have to do is take the first step and ask the Universe to lead you, and it will do so a step at a time.

Ch. 7: Your Purpose Gives You Clarity and Power

The Six Powers of Purpose is a conceptual framework I created to add clarity and power and to the process of getting in alignment with Divine Will.

If at this point, you are not already convinced of the importance of discovering and living your life's purpose, this chapter seeks to erase any hesitation once and for all. It begins with the first Power, The Power of Who You Are, then looks at the five remaining powers of your Purpose which build upon it.

Ch. 8: Claim Your Purpose and Passion Now

The chapter discusses how to blossom where you are, no matter how far out of alignment you currently feel with your purpose. We discuss the importance of acceptance as the first step to transformation, and of a daily gratitude practice to keep your focus where it needs to be – because what you focus on expands. Tips are Included for coming up with small, do-able steps that will lead you to the life of your dreams, and examples of how to get from here to there. How to create a life that has you leaping out of bed in the morning, starting now?

Ch. 9: Are You Ready

This chapter explores what it will take for you to show up in a way that manifests a life of Purpose, through questions such as:

- Are you ready for what could show up in your life?
- How will you know when you are living your purpose and your dream?
- How do you feel and think when you are living your purpose?

This chapter also encourages you to develop a Personal Mission Statement so you can journey forward with a compass to help you align each choice you make with your life's purpose. To this end, I share my Personal Mission Statement with you, that perhaps it may create a path forward for you to create yours.

Ch. 10: The Time is Now

One of the easiest ways to align your life with your purpose is to create a list of small activities that make your heart sing, and choose one of these to carry out each day. These activities should take no more than a half hour of your time and should be things that you can conceivably do on any average day. It could be something as simple as writing a letter to a cherished friend, writing in your journal, drawing or painting a scene in nature, or going for a run with your dog. What's important is that when you do this activity, you feel connected to your passion, optimism and wellbeing: the hallmarks of a life lived on purpose.

Living a life of purpose is about giving, but you cannot give what you do not have. This is why cultivating true Self-love is so important.

We all have subconscious blocks to receiving the love that we want and deserve, blocks that prevent us from choosing our highest and best good without our even realizing it. This is why if you really want to live your purpose, it is important to be willing to give up those parts of your subconscious identity that are keeping you from being the love that you are.

This can be scary at first, but there are many tools and techniques that can help, some of which I use in my work with my clients. When you release negative beliefs about yourself and the world the love that is who you truly are can shine through, and this automatically leads to a life lived on purpose.

Conclusion: Today is the First Day of the Rest of Your Life

I invite you to work with me, Neslyn, to be the Powerful You – this is the title of the sister book to this one. I want you to have the feeling of being inspired, knowing how to influence your passion and purpose so that you have the impact that you are here to create. Start today by joining my webinars and work with me even more deeply to make the contribution that only you can make in this life. That is why you are so unique and so special.

CHAPTER ONE

Arriving at a Life of Purpose

I am here for a purpose and that purpose is to grow into
a mountain, not to shrink to a grain of sand. Henceforth,
I will apply all my efforts to become the highest
mountain of all and I will strain my potential until it
cries for mercy.

— Og Mandino

Within my coaching practice I have had the privilege of working with high flying executives who have had what could be described as a successful career, yet deep within is the nagging question, Is there more? What is my life purpose here on this planet?

I believe that you are here for a purpose; you are not created at random. You are created for a definite purpose in life, and so is every other person in the world; this is the natural order of things. Each and every one of us has an equally important purpose.

I have learned that the secret to finding your purpose, is to realise that it is about being of service: your purpose is about giving, rather than receiving. What is interesting is that when you live the purpose for which you were created, the creator gives to you your highest and best good. That is, when you give the gifts that only you can give, you receive your deepest heart's desire. In this sense, when you are truly living your purpose, giving and receiving become one. When you are working in alignment with your purpose all aspects of your life are healed, you feel happier, healthier and even your finances improve.

In contrast when you are not working in alignment with your purpose, there is a chronic nagging anxiety because you unconsciously know that you are missing the mark. This can lead to unhealthy behaviours.

So Why Might We Not Be Clear About Our Purpose?

Simply, the way we were brought up does have an effect. If we were encouraged to live our joy, then we tend to be more in alignment with our purpose and that which is meaningful for us. If we were heavily steered in a particular direction to satisfy our family needs and our community's expectations we may never be fully aligned with our purpose. Purpose tells us why life is worth living, purpose helps us to define our values.

(*Nemko, Edwards, & Edwards*, 1998) in their study reveals that more than 46% of men and 40% of women say they are still trying to figure out the meaning and purpose of their life. *Daybre* (1999) notes that for most people, the number one problem is trying to figure out what they really want to do with their lives. *"From the time we are born, we are on a search to discover our life purpose. Most people never do find it. Yet there is a void, an emptiness until we discover our purpose in life."*

I believe that your creator has hard wired your life's purpose within you, and this purpose is unique to you and it enables you to help others and to feel emotional rewards.

That said, I believe that ultimately, achievement and fulfilment have very little to do with your education or skill level per se. Rather, it is about exploring who you are here to be and pursuing the kind of work that this leads you to do. That is how I define purpose, and I will expand upon this idea in the pages to come. For now I would like to share my story with you, as it illustrates clearly the power of knowing your purpose in life. As you will see, it can quite literally be a matter of life or death!

My Story

I have learnt that my dreams will keep calling me, and the question "Why am I here?" will not be satisfied unless I stay aligned and engaged with my purpose and my personal destiny.

— Neslyn Watson Druée

My own journey to a life of purpose and passion has continued to surprise me. Decades ago when I was first beginning my career, I never could have imagined myself

3

doing the work I do now, much less predicted it! My life's work evolved over time from providing health care as a nurse to providing mental, emotional and spiritual care as a coach helping others live their dreams and achieve success as they define it. For me there is no greater joy than empowering others to uncover their purpose and live their lives in congruence with it.

I am passionate about what I do, and by the time I reached age 63 in 2012, I had already achieved a lot and felt I was living a purposeful life in many ways. As I considered whether I might now be ready for retirement however, I thought about the legacy I wanted to leave and knew there was still much for me to do. I went about donating all the money I had to members of my community in London, in an effort to give the black community here more opportunities to achieve their dreams and expand their potential.

That felt good, yet as I worked in my garden afterwards a voice within my heart said, *'your greatest work is yet to be done, and you need to write.'* Of course my students have always asked me when I would write books on what I teach, and I have already published several. Yet I could not ignore this inner voice that urged me to write even more, to further explore and share the life lessons I have gained in my many years spent serving others and exploring these topics for myself. That moment in my garden was the genesis of the book you now hold.

A Matter of Life or Death

I knew that was really the only purpose of life: to be our self, live our truth, and be the love that we are.
— Anita Moorjani in Dying to Be Me: My Journey from Cancer, to Near Death, to True Healing

Let me get right to the point: I cannot emphasize enough how important it is to always, *always* listen to this voice that guides you from within. It may very well be a matter of life and death, as the following story from my own life illustrates in a powerful way.

The month of December 2013 found me on an operating table with a surgeon about to perform an operation for which I had already signed the consent form. Medical students had gathered to observe, and the anaesthetist was preparing to anesthetize me. It was a terrifying moment: changes had been discovered in a large polyp within my bowel that was now feared to be cancerous, and the operation I was about to undergo was risky. As a nurse, I was perhaps even more aware of the risk I was about to face than another person might be. At the very least, a section of my colon might have to be removed, leaving me with a colostomy bag for life.

As the anaesthetist took my arm to put me under however, a surprising calm befell me and I heard my voice call out to the surgeon: "Doctor, I don't want you to do the planned operation. I want you to do it by colonoscopy instead.' Aghast, the doctor replied with, "Neslyn, it can't be done. Your bowel will rupture, it's too high up." I knew very well that a ruptured bowel could be deadly, yet again I heard myself say with a calm not of this world: "Doctor I have prayed, your hands will be guided and my body is prepared. I will sign another consent form accepting the risk, please go ahead." So I signed the form just moments before surgery began, and the doctor performed it by colonoscopy in accordance with my request.

The fact that I am here to write this is proof that the operation was successful, and as a result I did not need to have a colostomy. What's more, the post-operative tissue analysis showed me to be free of cancer. It was the best possible outcome in a situation that could very well have turned life-threatening, and I believe that in that decisive moment, it was my purpose that kept me alive. The highest part of me that knows my reason for being on Earth simply knew that my time was not yet up, and that the riskier operation would therefore be successful.

Re-connecting With That Still, Small Voice

*And after the earthquake a fire; but the LORD was not
in the fire: and after the fire a still small voice.*

— I Kings 19:12, King James Bible

I love this verse from the Bible, because it shows so clearly how even raw elemental forces like earthquakes and fires cannot match the power of the voice of truth within you.

This was the voice that spoke through me on the operating table, and it is the voice that will lead you to your purpose. Most of us lose touch with this voice over time, yet much depends on recovering our ability to hear it. It may even be said that everything depends on it! Allow me to explain.

I believe that we are all born with a powerful inner guidance system, but too many of us are taught to ignore it early in life. The problem is that each time we dismiss this voice its volume gets lower and lower, until we cannot hear it at all. This is a great tragedy, for this still, small voice is none other than the voice of your inner truth. The tendency to ignore this voice is the reason why so many of us arrive at a certain point in life and find that our lives do not look at all like we expected them to. If you choose to believe what society tells you about what will make you happy rather than following what is true *for you*, you will be confused when you achieve those things and find that happiness still eludes you. Yet the answers have been within you all along—so how can you recover your ability to hear them?

From infancy we are taught to value logic and the mind above all else, and we learn to ignore our inner guidance system because *very often, its messages are not logical.* Think about it: have you ever received an inner message that you either ignored or listened to, and noted the consequences later? Almost everyone I have worked with has been able to recall at least one instance where this has happened to them, either for good or bad, and I believe there are many more that we forget entirely.

For example, did you ever get a strong nudge to not go out, but did so anyway and had a mishap of some kind? Conversely, did you ever listen to a nudge that told you to do something illogical, with miraculous results? You have likely heard stories of people who woke up the day of a long-planned vacation knowing that they shouldn't board the plane, which later crashed killing all aboard. There are many such stories about miraculous escape from disasters, synchronous meeting of one's true love, dream homes or job offers that come seemingly out of the blue, etc.

These are dramatic examples, and not everyone is destined to have such extreme experiences of their inner guidance system. However, I do believe that we all have access to this inner power, and that connecting with it is more than anything a matter of practice. My experience with my surgery suggests that listening to the voice of your inner truth may indeed be a matter of life or death in many instances, so why take a chance? The time to reconnect with that voice is now, and it all begins with the intention to do so.

Here are some practices that can help you recover your ability to hear the still, small voice of your higher self, which is the voice that will lead you to your purpose:

1. First, make a point of intending each morning to hear this guidance and act on it. This enhances your ability to notice those subtle hints from the universe, which then allows you to act upon them.

2. At the end of each day, record in a journal the messages you received, and what happened as a

result of your choice to act on them (or not). Doing this builds evidence for your mind that the still, small voice carries important information that should not be ignored. Be persistent with this practice, as it takes time to undo years of conditioning that have taught you to dismiss this inner voice. The process of learning to trust yourself cannot be rushed, but I assure you the results are well worth it.

3. Take a moment at intervals (e.g. weekly or monthly) to look back through your journal and acknowledge all the times that you have indeed listened. It is important not to skip this step, as it helps build the motivation you need to pursue further growth.

Your Intention And Attention Create Your Life

Intention and attention without tension creates fun.
— Neslyn Watson Druée

You may have heard it said that your intention and your attention create your life. I have certainly found this to be true, but I also find that many people take it too seriously. That is why I have coined my own version of this wisdom above, because what is the point of finding your purpose and passion if you don't have fun along the way? Yes you must recognize the power of your thoughts, but remember too that joy is your birth-right, and that sometimes living your best life is more about allowing than it is about hard work.

What do I mean when I speak of intention and attention? If you ask the average person for their definition of the word intention, their answer will usually involve the intention to do something. This is the norm in our culture, but I believe that a more powerful definition of intention refers to it as a state of being. Quite simply, intention as it relates to co-creation refers to *who you are being* on average in your daily life. Your being state dictates the power of your intention, and then your attention is what brings your ideas into concrete form.

In my work as a coach, I find that many people react to this news with a certain amount of bewilderment, if not outright dismay. If it is my state of being that does more than anything else to create my reality, they tell me, then what does that knowledge do for me? You see, we are not taught in this culture that we indeed have the power to alter who we are being, but I assure you that this is in fact the truth.

When you find yourself stuck in life, it is often because you hold limiting beliefs that keep you from seeing possibilities that may be right in front of you. You are constantly creating the circumstances in your world by virtue of the beliefs that you hold to be true, whether for good or ill. Most people are creating their lives from beliefs that live deep within their unconscious mind, unaware of the ways in which they hold themselves as victims of their situations and circumstances. This is why it is vitally important to address the subconscious when you are really seeking transformation, and there are a number of tools and techniques that can facilitate that.

Successful people know that energy goes where attention is, and they create their reality from what they put their attention on, both within and without. Your life will always express what is going on deep inside you, so ask yourself this:

Do realise that you are part of God's creation, which is perfect, and that you are therefore also perfect? Over and over again, I have seen that a lack of self-regard—indeed of *love* for self—is what most holds us back from living a life of purpose. Remember that Divinity is within you, and that just as God's creation unfolds, so what is right for you can unfold with equal ease. Know that absolutely no power on Earth can stop what is meant for you from coming your way, if you will just allow it.

So how do you allow it? The answer is as simple as it is difficult to do sometimes: love yourself. You must be the love that you are in order to align with your soul's purpose, and you can't do that if you are criticizing yourself all the time. Here are some practices to help you cultivate greater self-love:

1. Pay attention to the way you talk to yourself in your own head. Each time you say something to yourself, ask yourself "would I ever say this to someone I loved, or even to a perfect stranger?" If not, you certainly don't want to be saying it to yourself!

2. If you can, take a moment right then to write the thought down on paper, then burn it or tear it up.

This will help release the pattern of self-destructive and over-critical thinking. If you are not able to do that for any reason, simply imagine stamping the thought with the word CANCEL in big red letters. Writing is always more powerful, but this will do in a pinch.

3. Write a list every day of what you are grateful for, ending with *at least three lines of what you are grateful for about yourself.* It can be your good health, your kind heart, the talent you have for music—anything at all. It helps to start your list with things that you find easy to be grateful for, as this will raise your vibration enough to allow you to access those things you are grateful for about yourself. Persist with this practice, and it will change your life!

Everything You Most Want Is Inside You

True Power is within, and it is available now.
— Eckhart Tolle in Practicing the Power of Now

When you are truly purposeful about something, there is nothing that can keep it from you, for you are allowing Divine will to be done through you. When your heart's deepest desire is aligned with your vision and purpose, the things you desire will be drawn naturally and easily to you. This is the power of living your passion.

I wish to end this chapter by emphasising that everything you could ever want or need exists already within you. How is this possible, you ask? It is not only possible, but inevitable, because in truth it is never a concrete outcome that we desire; it is the feeling that we believe that outcome will bring us that we truly want. Standing in your power is about being on purpose, being aligned with the highest part of yourself, and knowing both your humanity and your Divinity as a result.

Your life purpose is an expression of your soul's reason for incarnating on this planet at this time—in a sense, it is an intention statement for your whole life. It thus applies to every aspect of your life, not only your work, and it is the compass that allows you to discern how to best use your limited time on this planet.

I firmly believe that the greatest contribution each of us can make in our life and work is to live in accordance with our purpose. When we do, we not only find great fulfilment for ourselves, but we become a beacon for others. The tragedy is that most people never take the time to reflect on their purpose: indeed, less that 1% of people can articulate why they are here.

In the same way that you may have taken on the judgements of others in the form of limiting beliefs, you may have also chosen to believe that it is not important to know your purpose, if you even have one. This is just another aspect of the back-to-front thinking that forms the dominant worldview on the planet today. From an early age, society and the media condition you to believe that happiness lies in the acquisition of things, when in fact the things we most desire—love, fulfilment, a sense of belonging—can only be found within.

So the question is, how long are you going to wait? Will you begin the work necessary to learn and live your purpose today, or will you continue to accept a life of mediocrity? While your purpose is always there for you to discover, I contend that you must not wait for it to reveal itself. You must hold a strong intention to uncover the treasure within, for you never know, it just might save your life!

CHAPTER TWO

Joy Is Your Birth Right

The privilege of a lifetime is being who you are.

— Joseph Campbell

So far I have laid out where your life's purpose comes from and how you may uncover what it is. I've explained that you have a purpose that is unique to you, and which you fulfil by giving the gifts that only you can give to the world. Yet I feel it is important not to stop there in your exploration of what precisely is meant by purpose, because exploring and deepening your understanding of what purpose is will enhance your ability to be who you came into this life to be. In my work as a coach, I have learnt that **joy** is available to each and every one of us—indeed it is our birthright—and that joy is what we experience when we truly live our **purpose** and **passion**.

The relationship between these three subjects—joy, purpose and passion—is the subject of this book and has become the cornerstone of my work as a coach. If you think you already know what each of these terms mean, I encourage you to keep reading with an open mind and really consider what I share here. You may be surprised to find that expanding your understanding of these terms will in turn expand the level of fulfilment that you are able to experience in your life.

> *True inner joy is self-created.*
> *It does not depend on outer circumstances.*
> *A river is flowing in and through you carrying the message of joy.*
> *This divine joy is the sole purpose of life.*

— Sri Chinmoy

The Inner and Outer Purpose of Your Life

Your creator cannot fulfil your dreams if you do not have a dream. Your creator cannot bless your purpose if you do not engage in the purpose for your life. Your creator cannot help you fulfil your goal if you do not have a goal. So it is important for you to co-create with your creator. It is important for you to know what makes your heart sing, what gives you joy.

> *To know yourself as the Being underneath the thinker, the stillness underneath the mental noise, the love and joy underneath the pain, is freedom, salvation, enlightenment.*

— Eckhart Tolle

Take a moment now to simply focus on your breath. Don't judge it or try to change it; simply observe your own natural breathing rhythm and marvel at this and the myriad other mundane miracles that make your life possible. This is one of the simplest and most effective practices that I know of to get in touch with the expansive consciousness that you truly are, underneath your pain, mental constructs, and problems. As the quote above suggests, who you truly are is this subtle stillness and joy, which exists above and beyond anything you may or may not do.

Some of you reading this may feel a sense of confusion at this statement, for you may still be thinking of your life's purpose as something you *do*. Remember, however, my exploration of the concept of intention in the last chapter: in my view, it is best thought of as a state of being, rather than something you do. If your purpose is an intention statement for your whole life, then it follows that your purpose may be more about being than doing.

But clearly life requires action of each of us—we must engage in what the Buddha called 'right action' in order to align our lives with who we truly are. So how can we be sure that the actions we take are expressions of our highest and best selves? How can we remain in touch with the stillness within, even as we take action to achieve our aims?

The answer is simple, but far from easy: presence. I believe that simply cultivating presence through practices like mindfulness is one of the most powerful things each of us can do to live a more joyful and purposeful life. The reason is that all of the answers to your most deeply held questions lie within you. No one else can tell you why you are here; you must make the effort to connect with the innermost part of your being, where the answer to this question may be found.

Wise people have spoken of these things for millennia, but I believe that the unprecedented times we live in call for an updated approach to living 'in the world, but not of it.' In his best-selling book *The Power of Now*, spiritual teacher Eckhart Tolle offers such an approach when he describes how each of us has both an inner and an outer aspect to our life purpose. He writes:

> *Your life's journey has an outer purpose and an inner purpose. The outer purpose is to arrive at the goal or destination, to accomplish that which you set out to do. The outer purpose belongs to the horizontal dimension of space and time. The inner purpose concerns a deepening of your being in the vertical dimension of the timeless Now. Your outer journey may contain a million steps; your inner journey only has one; the step you are taking Now. As you become more deeply aware of this step... the light of Being will shine through. This is the purpose and the fulfilment of your inner journey, the journey into yourself.*

Your purpose is defined by who you came to this life to be—that is, your soul's intention for your life. We tend to think of our identities as more or less static, but this passage makes clear that *you get to choose each and every moment who you are being Now.* I find this an exciting prospect, for it highlights the fact that you have full power to choose who you are being in response to the life circumstances you are faced with. This is, in fact, the only thing you *can* control: who you choose to be in the face of our life circumstances, and how you respond to the things that happen to you.

So if you find yourself struggling with a decision or simply unsure of how to proceed, ask yourself this question: which choice will allow me to be my authentic self? Which do I feel will lead me closer to my highest and best path? Here are some techniques for connecting with your purpose at any moment:

1. Ask yourself the following question any time you are faced with a choice or feel adrift: "If I were truly committed to my highest and best good, what would I do?" This is also an excellent prompt to use for journaling, as a way to clarify your desires and intentions at any given time. It is especially powerful first thing in the morning, as you set an intention for your day.

2. There is a part of you that always knows your truth. You can call on this wisdom by observing how you feel when you imagine making a particular choice. Do you feel a sense of expansion in your body, or contraction? Do you feel energized or drained when you say, 'I choose to (fill in the blank)?' Learn to trust the answers you receive—they will never fail you.

3. Most of all, use breath awareness and any other technique that resonates with you to *stay present*. It is almost impossible to hear your inner voice of truth, much less act on it, if you are not present. Therefore make becoming present your first step when using any technique in this book.

Your Life Is What You Make Of It

Life doesn't happen to you, it happens for you.

— Jim Carrey

Each and every moment presents you with an opportunity to express your authentic self. The question I would like to ask you is this: what if life is not happening *to* you, but is instead happening *for* you? What if the events that you consider obstacles are in fact perfect opportunities for you to learn and grow, hand-delivered by the Universe in response to your soul's request? Pause for a moment to really let that sink it, because this idea will change your life if you let it. What if a part of you fervently asked for every experience you have had, in order to release what no longer serves and step into a new level of experience? How would your response to your life's events change if you knew this to be true beyond all doubt?

Joseph Campbell put it this way:

Life has no meaning. Each of us has meaning and we bring it to life. It is a waste to be asking the question when you are the answer.

It might be a bit jarring at first to hear such a respected philosopher assert that 'life has no meaning,' but at its core this message is one of profound hope. Why? Well, if there is no absolute meaning to life, that means that you do not have to try to conform to what others say life is about if it does not resonate for you. You now have permission to live life on your own terms and strive for success as *you* define it! This is important, because the tendency to discount what is personally meaningful to us in deference to what society tells us we 'should' want is at the root of the crises of meaning that many people experience at one time or another.

The point is that your experience of meaning is not fixed—you get to choose. You can choose to view life's challenges from the perspective of victimhood, believing that life is out to get you, or you can choose to see each challenge as a blessing in disguise. You can choose to believe that your life experiences come to you for a reason, even if that reason is beyond your comprehension at this time. You can choose to believe that life will never give you more than you are able to handle, and that what you most want lies on the other side of your fear.

If you want, you can even start to welcome the unknown as a source of blessings beyond imagining, rather than a source of things to be feared. It is a wonderful moment when you realise that the unknown is at least as likely to spring gifts on you as it is to bring you difficulties, because then you know that the sky's the limit! This is a major turning point, because you now know that it is safe to let go of control (which is an illusion anyway) and allow the universe to bring you what is truly yours. Then life really becomes fun because you still have the power of intention and attention, but the tension caused by an irrational fear of the unknown has melted away. (Remember the formula I mentioned earlier: *Intention + Attention – Tension = Fun!*)

So how can you begin to embrace the gifts the unknown offers and squeeze every last drop of learning from life? Here are some suggestions:

1. This may surprise you, but the first step I would suggest is to commit to taking responsibility for at least some part of every experience you have ever had, positive or negative. This means forgiving yourself and others for negative events that happened in the past, especially if those events came seemingly 'out of the blue.' This is important because the charge the past holds for us is due more than anything to a lack of forgiveness—indeed, forgiveness is your key to freedom. It is not about condoning what anyone else did, it is about freeing *yourself* from the past.

   Even in those events that seem to consist entirely of another victimising you, you can always find at least some small piece to take responsibility for. It is important to feel safe during this process, so if you know this will be challenging for you I recommend undertaking it under the guidance of a professional counsellor or coach. It will be well worth it to do so, for only when you have fully forgiven yourself and others can you fully release your fear of the unknown. And only when you release your fear of the unknown can the universe bring you the life of your dreams.

2. Draw a timeline representing the decades of your life, marking '1' as your first decade, '2' as your second decade and so on. What were some challenges, difficulties and hardships you have overcome, or are in the process of overcoming? What have you noticed in regard to patterns? This practice helps with self-awareness as well as being an opportunity to acknowledge the growth you have already achieved. Remember that when you acknowledge how far you have already come, it fuels your desire to persist in your growth.

3. Think of your life as a film, and yourself as the person observing the film. This is an accurate metaphor for the relationship between your observer self (who you truly are) and your ego/personality as it goes through the experience of life.

Perhaps you have a favourite movie that you have enjoyed watching many times, even though you know everything that is going to happen and when. Realise that there is a part of you that does know the possible plotlines of your life, and is excited at the possibility of watching them unfold. Realise also that, while your soul may come in with a particular intention, it is your choices in each moment that determine the shape that the film of your life will finally take. Just remember what that observer part of you already knows—that you cannot get it wrong, and there is no such thing as a wasted life because *you can always make a different choice now.*

Have Faith In Yourself and Your Purpose

Faith is a gift from your creator. Every person lives by faith; when you drink a glass of water, you hold the faith that it is not contaminated, when you go across a bridge, you trust that it will support you. The key to faith in yourself is accepting that you are unique and powerful. Whatever you decide to be in life, whatever goals you decide to pursue, there is one vital thing that is crucial and that is to love and believe in yourself.

> *I encourage you to accept that you may not be able to see*
> *a path right now, but that doesn't mean it's not there.*
> — Nick Vujicic, *Life Without Limits*

There is an acronym that I often share with my coaching clients that I encourage them to think about every time fear arises: "FEAR is False Evidence Appearing Real." I love this idea because it really is true: the vast majority of the time, our fears have very little, if any, basis in reality. It is as if we are looking at a picture of a tiger and believing it is going to eat us!

This is where faith comes in, and here is what I have learned on that subject: even if you don't believe in a universal intelligence, you can still choose to trust life, for this is really just another aspect of trusting yourself. What's more, this is once again a simple matter of practice. As I discussed in the last chapter with regard to listening to the still, small voice within, your ability to trust that all is well will strengthen each time you choose to do so. Indeed, you *must* choose to trust over and over again in order to move beyond fear, for this is the only way to change a belief forever. Even a person with a very fear-based belief system can begin to shine if they choose over and over again to trust life and most of all, themselves.

In 2014, actor Jim Carrey gave a commencement speech at the Maharishi University of Management in which he shared the following wisdom on the subject of faith:

> *Take a chance on faith—not religion, but faith. Not hope, but faith. I don't believe in hope. Hope is a beggar. Hope walks through the fire. Faith leaps over it.*

To be clear, I feel that hope also serves a purpose when we are just beginning the journey from surviving to thriving. It can help start us on the path from victimhood to empowerment when faith is not yet accessible to us. But I also encourage you to recognise that while hope can be useful, it is faith that will take you where you *really* want to go, to that realm beyond your mind's ability to imagine where all your highest dreams live.

Embrace Where You Are Right Now

Acceptance is the first step to transformation.
— Neslyn Watson Druée

We tend to be more aligned to our purpose, and to that which has meaning for us, if we are encouraged at an early age to live our joy. If you were heavily steered in a particular career direction in order to satisfy your family's needs or your community's expectations, you can expect to have some difficulty in becoming fully aligned to your purpose. If this describes you, I encourage you to realise that if you are waiting for permission from others to shine your light, it will never come. In truth, the only permission you need to uncover and live your purpose is *your own*.

Where you are right now reflects every choice you have ever made, and your power lies in recognising and accepting that truth. You cannot go somewhere else if you do not first accept where you are now. Understand that wherever you are on this journey is totally fine, for it never ends. You can only start where you are, knowing that your commitment to living your purpose will inspire those around you. The only sure thing is that if you never start, you will never arrive.

Despite what some self-help authors would have you believe, the fact is that there is no single path to success and fulfilment that will work for everyone, because what works for you is as unique as you are. Your life's true meaning can only be found within, and you refine it as you grow. Your own inner resonance is the only true indicator of what the current expression of your life's purpose is, and whether you are living in alignment with it or not. In the end, you must cast all definitions aside and recognise that you are in alignment with your purpose whenever you are experiencing joy. What you do with your time will change throughout your life, but when you are in alignment with your joy, you are on purpose and it is the triumph of your soul. So I leave you with the following poem.

Joy! Joy! I triumph! Now no more I know
Myself as simply me. I burn with love
Unto myself, and bury me in love.
The centre is within me and its wonder
Lies as a circle everywhere about me.
Joy! Joy! No mortal thought can fathom me.
I am the merchant and the pearl at once.
Lo, Time and Space lie crouching at my feet.
Joy! Joy! When I would reveal in a rapture.
I plunge into myself and all things know.

— Attar

Translated by Margaret Smith, from *The Persian Mystics*

CHAPTER THREE

Where Passion and Purpose Meet

Follow your passion; it will lead you to your purpose.

— Oprah Winfrey

Without question, passion is both the gateway to and the hallmark of a purposeful life. People who do great feats often discover their life's calling by identifying what aroused their passion. For example, Mother Teresa was so passionate about helping street children in Kolkata that she chose to break the convention of living in a convent in order to forge a path of her own. Passion drives people of great purpose forward, giving them a compelling urge to discover what they were born to do.

What do you think of when you hear the word passion? For many of us, the honest answer is that our first association is with romantic passion—with the burning fire you feel for a special someone, especially at the start of the relationship. The thought of your beloved consumes you day and night, no matter what you are supposed to be doing, and when you finally see them again your whole world appears brighter.

You feel that you can do anything with your beloved by your side; your passion has unleashed the limitlessness of your spirit, and there is no going back.

Except that too often, we do go back. Sooner or later, the intensity of that passionate fire diminishes until only embers are left, and these embers may not be sufficient to sustain the relationship unless you work to build them up again. If you are like most people, you are dismayed to discover that it takes real effort to keep the fire alive, and a moment of truth inevitably arrives: do you have what it takes to stay committed, or do you feel you would be better off parting ways? It is rarely an easy question to answer, but answer it you must if you wish to stay true to yourself.

What is the relationship, then, between romantic passion and the kind of passion that will lead you to your life's purpose? While they may seem unrelated at first, they are united in a powerful way: they both live in the heart.

We spend so much time honing our minds, acquiring the latest knowledge and skills to further our goals, but how much time have you devoted to healing and expanding your heart? Just as we feel a strong sensation in the area of our heart when we are passionately in love, so too do we feel this sensation when we are *doing what we love*. This wonderful sensation is part of your built-in guidance system, and it tells you when you are on the right track from your soul's perspective. Why, then, do so few of us make use of it?

The reasons are unique to each individual, but the most common ones are emotional trauma that creates fear, societal conditioning or need, and a sense of obligation. These forces close down our hearts to what we love over time. Often, it happens so slowly that you do not even realise what is taking place until one day you find yourself wondering why you are alive. Your heart becomes small, crowded out by other things that you have given more importance to. This leads to a sense of existential despair, a perception that life has lost its meaning. What is interesting is that because you do not know how you arrived at this dark place, you do not know how to get out of it, either.

Get In Touch With What You Love

> *Love is the essential reality and our purpose on earth. To be consciously aware of it, to experience love in ourselves and others, is the meaning of life. Meaning does not lie in things. Meaning lies in us.*
>
> — Marianne Williamson

So if you find yourself in this dispirited place, what can you do to turn things around? At its core, the journey to purpose and passion is one of returning your awareness to the unique expression of love that only you can offer the world. This is why self-love is so important, and it starts with renewing your relationship with your heart. You must undertake the task of remembering what it is you most love, and make space for those things in your life again.

If this sounds overwhelming, know that even the smallest step in this direction will have ripple effects throughout your life. Why? Let's review some basic universal truths:

1. God is love.
2. You are a child of God.
3. Therefore, you are love.
4. Therefore, the secret to life is to express the love that you are.

I want to say this again, because it is so very important: love is not something you do, and it is not just an emotion: it is *who you fundamentally are*. We are each, at our core, here to express love in a way that no other being in the Universe can do. This means that when you really get in touch with what you love—when you see it, claim it, and commit to it—there is no way you will not receive that which you most desire. It must be so, for in committing to being your true self in this way you are aligning yourself with what might be called the will of God, and *there is nothing more powerful than that.*

> *Another way to say this is that your results will always match your true intentions.*

So ask yourself, are my intentions aligned with the love that I am, with my highest purpose that only I can know? Your life can only reflect to you what is going on deep inside you. Realise that you are part of God's creation, which is perfect, and therefore you yourself are also perfect, just as you are. This is a central paradox of life: that we are each perfect in our Divinity, even as we are imperfect in our humanity. This understanding will not make your problems disappear, but it will do a great deal to help your evolution become a source of pleasure rather than pain.

The Creator is Divine, so Divinity is within you. God's creation unfolds, and what is right for you will unfold when you align yourself with Divine will. Know that nothing, absolutely nothing; no other power can stop what is meant for you. When you are truly purposeful about something, there is nothing that can keep it from you. When your heart's deepest desire is aligned with your vision and purpose, the things you desire will be drawn naturally and easily to you.

Standing in your power is about being on purpose and being aligned with the highest part of yourself, knowing both your humanity and your Divinity. As Joseph Campbell observed so profoundly, when you are on purpose and follow your bliss, doors will be opened where you would not imagine there would be doors.

Here are some questions and exercises to help you re-align your thoughts and actions with the wisdom of your heart. Write down the answers that come to you in a journal, so you can return to it at any time. Be sure not to edit yourself, but let what comes flow unimpeded in a stream-of-consciousness style. It is amazing the wisdom you can bring through you when you let go of controlling the flow of your thoughts.

1. What makes your heart sing? Put another way, what are the unique ways to access joy that work for you? List out at least ten activities that really make you happy and in which you can 'lose yourself.' It can be anything, from swimming or playing music to teaching or traveling. At least some of them—the majority in fact—should be things that you can reasonably do on any given day. The less time they take the better, because I'm going to ask you to commit to actually doing at least one of them every day, no matter how busy you are.

   For example, if one of yours is outdoor adventure, can taking a walk in the woods near your home serve the same purpose as climbing a mountain in a foreign land? The most important thing is to find ways to tap into your joy each and every day.

   Once you have your list, here is the next step: write each one down on its own small slip of paper, then place all the slips together in a jar. At the start of each day, you can now select a paper at random and commit to doing that item today, even if only for 10 minutes. I encourage you to do this first thing, because then the chances that you will actually make time for it are much improved.

2. Who inspires you, and why? Really dig deep with this one, and journal extensively to get to the bottom of it, for it will show you what your most deeply-held values are. What's more, the qualities you

admire in others also exist in you; they must, or you wouldn't even be able to see them! Spend some time considering why you are inspired by these people and acknowledge the places where the essence they carry also lives in you.

3.   When you were a child, what did you always want to do or be? I have found that even people who had difficult childhoods can usually find at least one memory of being in the flow and losing track of time in one pursuit or another. It may be that the feeling state is more important, such as the feeling you had on Christmas mornings, and that is okay too. The point is to regain your connection with who you were before you took on outside influences and shut down your light. This part of you still exists, and has been waiting patiently to come out again and play!

4.   When and where do you feel closest to your creator? Another way to say this is, when do you most strongly feel a loving presence in your life? For some of us it may be in church or community, for others it may be solitude in nature. You are looking for the places and experiences that most help you connect with the Love that you are.

5.   As a follow up to number 4 above, when in your life do you feel a sense of awe and wonder? How can you tap into those feelings more of the time?

6. If you knew the service you were here to give to the Earth and all sentient beings, what would that service be? In what ways do you feel called to be of service to others? What patterns in the overall trace of your life might point you to this?

7. As a follow-up to number 6 above, who are the people, past and present, who in your view have made the greatest contribution? Why? In a similar way to question number 2 above, those qualities that you admire in these people also exist in you, and their most deeply-held values and motivations likely mirror your own.

8. When and where do you feel in the flow of life? Is there anything that consistently makes you lose track of time when you do it?

9. What do you feel would give you the greatest feeling of accomplishment in life? Are you doing it now? What steps could you take to spend more of your time doing that?

10. What would make you leap out of bed each morning? What goals can you set that feel that exciting to you?

11. How do you personally define success, and who would you have to be to have that? Notice I did not say, 'what would you have to do to get it,' but rather 'who would you have to be?' This is quite intentional, because it is your state of being (your mindset, if you will) that determines more than

anything what you allow yourself to have. This is a big subject that we will explore in much more detail in subsequent chapters, but just ponder it for now and see what it brings up for you.

12. There is a simple, elegant tool created by Janet Attwood called The Passion Test. I encourage you to consider taking this test, as it can help you hone in on your most deeply-held values and passions very quickly. More information can be found at www.thepassiontest.com.

We will revisit these questions numerous times throughout the book, so be sure to keep your journal handy as you continue reading. You may also wish to bookmark or photocopy this page, so you can review these questions any time you feel the need to refresh your commitment to living on purpose. It is important when embarking on a course of transformation to set yourself up for success, and reviewing these questions often is one way to do this.

Where Your Joy and Service Meet

Don't ask yourself what the world needs. Ask yourself what makes you come alive, and then go do it. Because what the world needs is people who have come alive.

— Howard Thurman

Your purpose speaks to you via your passion, which shows you what you love to do. It speaks to your heart and draws your attention to what gives you joy, to those things that your heart feels passionate about. The more time you can devote to these things, and the more you can raise your consciousness and let go of fear, the more your life will begin to reflect your purpose at every level.

It has been said that we are spiritual beings having a physical experience. It has also been said that the heart is the doorway to the spirit. As I noted earlier, your purpose can be thought of as an intention statement for your whole life. It is a statement of the larger wisdom behind why you exist, the reason for your being on this planet now. Within your purpose lies the intention of why you came into being, and the worthwhile markers for a meaningful life.

Living in your purpose means that you live with passion, because living your passion is how your spirit—the God in you, you could say—creates its fullest expression in the world. Remember what I said earlier in this chapter? You are a child of God, and your life is an expression of Divine will. When you realise this, all doubt melts away because you know that your deepest desires are already granted. Free will is the law of the Universe, but our deepest will and the Will of God are always one and the same.

There is another vital truth that follows from this, and it is this: that your most purpose-driven life will always be driven by the desire to serve others. This is simply a natural expression of your higher consciousness, which knows that in truth there is no separation between you and every other being in the universe. What is important is to remember that before you can serve others, *you must first serve yourself.*

Let that idea sink in for a moment. Does it surprise you? If so, know that living a life of true purpose will require you to let go of some out-dated beliefs regarding your own self-worth. Think about it: you cannot give to another what you do not have yourself. Since this is true, it follows that you can best serve others when you first give to yourself. This represents a radical change in mind-set for many people, but in my experience (and that of my clients) it is well worth the effort to change it.

This truth tells us that when you really align with your soul's highest purpose, abundance will flow your way. Indeed, the more you recognise that giving and receiving are one and the same, the more will come to you, so that you may better serve others. This is why I know that purpose, passion and abundance can all be yours—indeed, if you will but have the courage to follow your heart, they must be!

Are you ready, then, to commit to your passions? It starts with you healing your heart so you can give yourself the love you need and deserve, instead of waiting for someone else to appear and magically bestow it on you. That alone is a revolutionary thought for many people, especially women! What if it has never been anyone else's job to give you what you need, but it is you yourself who are best qualified to give it? How would your relationship with yourself have to change to allow that to happen?

I am here to tell you that it is possible to get from here to there, that I have witnessed many of my clients choose this journey and create the life of their dreams as a result. The question is, who are you really, and how much longer are you going to wait? The answers lie in your passions and what they reveal about who you are and why you are here.

Let Your Passion Lead

What you seek is seeking you.

— Jalaluddin Rumi

Passion is a wonderfully personal experience. There is no telling where it will lead you, but I will say that when you really follow it, it will take you to heaven on Earth as you define it. When you begin to do what you love, engaged with the activities and pursuits that make your heart expand, you will find your life being pulled in directions that you cannot now begin to imagine. This can feel scary, but like skydiving or any similar activity, when you are able to let go and trust it becomes exhilarating!

You come to know that magic is real when you open your heart to your purpose and passion. If you took some time to answer the questions earlier in this chapter, you now have at least some idea of where your passions lie. Now all that remains is to take concrete steps to align yourself with your purpose, what some have called your 'soul's code.' But where to begin? The prospect can seem overwhelming at best or impossible at worst, but I am here to remind you that the journey of a thousand miles begins with a single step!

If you are like many people, you may now feel bogged down with questions about how to bring greater joy, passion and purpose into your life. You may be saying to yourself: how will I find the money? How will I master the skill? How will I make a success of this at this stage of my life?

In response to those concerns, I would like to share another fabulous quote from that same commencement speech by Jim Carrey, who as it turns out is quite the sage as well as comedian. To the young people just starting out he had this to say:

> *Your job is not to figure out how it's going to happen for you, but to open the door in your head and when the doors open in real life, just walk through [them]. Don't worry if you miss your cue. There will always be another door opening.*

I am here to tell you from my own experience that this wisdom applies at any age: the important thing is never the 'how' it is, rather, the 'why.' The tapestry of your life is stitched together by a unifying, universal knowledge that is manifested from joy, and when you match that frequency, the events that transpire in your life will astound you.

In conclusion, here is my formula for uncovering your soul's highest Purpose:

Your Joy + Your Values + Your Values & Priorities + Service = Your Purpose

Take some time to play with this equation, and I mean it, have fun! If there is one thing I have learned in my long years spent developing myself and helping others do the same, it is that while the steps required of us may not always be fun, having fun is nonetheless a very good use of your time. I hope you are enjoying this book so far, and I encourage you to keep reading if you would like to continue the journey to purpose with me. It is my joy and privilege to join you in the discovery of how you wish to spend your precious time on this planet, and I appreciate your willingness to stick it out with me.

Let Go of What Keeps You From Living With Joy, Purpose and Passion

Freedom is not the absence of commitments, but the ability to choose—and commit myself to—what is best for me.

— Paulo Coelho, The Zahir

You have made it this far, and I want to congratulate you. Your willingness to read this book, and especially to begin this chapter, signals that you have already reached a critical level of commitment to living a life of purpose. At some level, you already know that the answers you seek are available to you, and that they can be found within. You are ready and willing to dig deep, to excavate the real reasons why you may not be living a life of joy, purpose and passion to the degree you could be.

I want to be straight with you: this passage we are about to navigate together may be uncomfortable at times. As your consciousness coach, I am going to ask you questions that are designed to help you uncover those deep, subconscious blocks that are preventing you from living the life you came to live. I am then going to share with you tools and techniques that can help you get through your fears, so you can begin living your joy, purpose and passion at a new level.

Remember that joy is your birthright and love is who you are; therefore it is in your power to release those patterns that no longer serve you, because *they are not you.* I often tell my clients that love brings up that which is unlike itself for the purpose of release, because I have observed it to be true. In a safe space that is held by someone whose intention is to serve your highest good, it becomes easy to release things that felt impossible to let go of on your own.

As we prepare to explore together the ways in which you are unknowingly preventing your dreams from manifesting in your life, I want you to remember that these blocks we will be looking at are *not personal.* By and large, the self-imposed internal limitations that are holding you back are the same ones that most of us human beings face to one degree or another, at one time or another in our lives. Remember this when you feel like a failure, knowing that in truth there is no such thing as failure, only opportunities to learn. No human being is a failure, but we are all—without exception—here to learn.

So, are you ready? Take a deep breath, and let us dive into this next leg of the journey together. You may be surprised at what it makes possible for you.

Create Yourself Anew Each And Every Day

Everything can be taken from a man but one thing: the last of the human freedoms—to choose one's attitude in any given set of circumstances, to choose one's own way.

— Viktor E. Frankl, Man's Search for Meaning

This process that I am about to lead you through can be compared to the process that a mother and child undergo during birth. Many people are surprised to learn that it is actually the foetus that initiates the birth process much of the time. When the time to be born becomes optimal—and this is unique to each case, within the 37-42 week period of term—the foetus begins to transfer proteins called telomeres to its mother via the placenta, and this in turn triggers her body to begin preparing for birth. The innate wisdom that creates each of us thus propels the process of birth into motion, and the child is eventually born.

This closely parallels the process of creating ourselves that each of us undergoes every day. If this idea is new to you, consider the following:

- The mental/emotional (vibrational) tone that you begin your day with will tend to persist throughout your day
- The tone you hold in each moment will colour your choices in that moment
- You can use the power of intention and affirmation to change your vibrational tone at any time

People in search of awakening (or success as they define it) have long asked sages and gurus to explain the relationship between effort and grace. Which is more important, they want to know: the effort that I put towards reaching my goals, or the moment that the hand of Providence moves in my favour, which is beyond my control? Do my actions really make a difference, or are forces beyond my understanding more responsible for the events of my life?

My answers to these questions relate to the childbirth analogy I outlined above. Since we are each individual sparks of the Divine, you could say that a 'moment of grace' is simply a moment of choice at the level of your spirit, and that a miracle is simply an instantaneous shift in consciousness that allows you to have a new reality. This is akin to the moment the birth process begins, when there is a subtle shift from the passive state of pregnancy to the active process of birth. That is, while in a sense everything depends on that initial spark of grace, your goals will not be achieved without a great deal of courage, hard work and perseverance.

As any mother will tell you, giving birth to a child is very hard work, and when it takes longer than you expect it to you may feel like giving up. Yet the entire process depends on that spark of grace, that signal from the universe that says 'yes, now is the time.' If you are reading this book, then you have already received something very important: grace in the form of a burning desire to do what it takes to live a life of joy, purpose and passion.

Think about that for a moment: if you are reading this, then *you are already the recipient of grace*. Not only that: if you feel a longing in your heart for something you cannot quite define, or if you are determined to change your station in life, then *you already have what it takes to reach your goals*. You already contain that which you seek; your task now is simply to water the seeds of your potential so that they can grow.

Any mother will tell you that while delivering a child is not easy, the rewards are so very worth it. So like childbirth, choosing to live a life of purpose is not without risk. It is also true, however, that the risk is greatly reduced by the presence of qualified helpers—doctors, nurses and midwives in the case of childbirth, or experienced teachers or coaches on the path of life transformation.

It is my goal as your coach to help you navigate the 'birth canal' of your life, so that like a new baby you may emerge safely into a bright new world. You create yourself and your life anew each day, and I am here to help you do that in a conscious way that makes you a magnet for your dreams. I have seen it work for many of my clients, so I know it can work for you, too.

So let me ask you this: why do you think that phrases like 'you create your own reality' resonate with so many people, yet so few of us experience our lives that way? The answer is that it resonates because it is true, but we don't experience ourselves as the authors of our own lives because *the vast majority of our choices are unconscious*. It is only when we are able to make the unconscious, conscious, that we begin to experience true empowerment in our lives.

It is my role as a consciousness coach to help people like you learn how to consciously create their lives by creating themselves anew each day. As the late, great Wayne W. Dyer once said, "you don't get what you want, you get what you are." Your task, then, is to align who you are being in each moment with the vision that you wish to manifest in the world.

It is a simple law of physics that when two frequencies are too different from one other, they cannot interact; this is also known as the Law of Attraction. Therefore, if who you are currently being (that is, your overall vibration) is at odds with who you would need to be in order to have the life you want, you can be certain that nothing is going to change. This is why regardless of your specific goals, the foundation of your efforts must be inner work to change your vibration.

I will say that it is much easier to accomplish this with the support of a qualified coach who can create a safe container in which to do the work. That said, there are tools you can use on your own that, when applied consistently and with enthusiasm, have the power to help you make real change. Here are a few that have proven especially powerful for my clients:

1. *Affirmation.* Affirmation is a practice that trains your brain to function in a different vibrational groove than the one it is used to, and when practiced with enthusiasm on a daily basis it can be remarkably

effective. It is especially beneficial when done in the morning, as a way to set the tone for your day.

Just remember that a good affirmation is just that: *a statement affirming the desired goal as already accomplished.* Your subconscious mind does not recognize negative statements, so if your affirmation is "I am not in resistance", it will hear "I am in resistance" and this is what you will get. In this case, if you rather use the words "I am in the flow of productive co-creation" as your affirmation, your chances of checking off some to-dos are much improved!

2. *Writing to Release.* If you are human, you have negative thoughts—remember, it's not personal! You need a way to release them so that the light of your higher self can begin to shine through. Remember that your thoughts are not who you are, but they will create your experience if you let them, and this tool provides a way to take charge of the thoughts you let into your head.

First, take a sheet of paper and write at the top, 'What I Am Letting Go Of.' Underneath this, get out all your emotions, taking care not to censor yourself: the point of this exercise is to stop suppressing these emotions and get them all *out*. Write down not only what it is you are upset about, but also the names of everyone involved, being sure to include 'myself' and 'God' on the list, for in essence they are one and the same! Don't be surprised if some of what you write seems to come out of nowhere, as the 'friends and relations' of the first thoughts that come to mind are pulled into the paper. Think to yourself that this is not just an exercise; you are really, truly placing the energy of these thoughts in the paper once and for all.

When you feel complete, fold the paper over and write something like "I forgive myself and everyone involved, thank you God for transforming this now" on the back.

Finally—and this is the most important step—*burn or shred the paper*. Really feel these thoughts leave your mind as you do so. This is a good practice to do at the end of every day, just to clear any negativity that you may have unknowingly accumulated. It is good to do it in the morning also, especially if you wake up feeling 'off.'

Commit to doing this practice each and every day for just one week and see what happens! You may be surprised at what begins to happen for you as a result of making more space for the Love that you are to shine through.

3. *Say Yes to Life*. This practice is so simple, but sometimes it is one of the most powerful ones you can undertake. In a way, it is an updated version of gratitude practice that really starts with seeing (and believing in) all the good that is already surrounding

you. It is a good one to try when you are feeling really stuck, after writing to release. There are a number of ways to employ it:

- You can take a short walk in which you mentally repeat the word 'yes' to yourself the entire time, intending as you do so to release all resistance to what the universe is trying to bring you.
- You can repeat the word 'yes' while visualizing your goals.
- You can look in the mirror and say things like 'yes, I am worthy,' or 'yes, I am loved.'

Just choose what works for you in any given situation. The point is that we often don't realize when we are unconsciously saying 'no' to our manifestations in one way or another, and this practice counteracts that tendency.

Some of my clients who have read about the Law of Attraction have a twisted idea of gratitude when they first come to me: they think of it as something you do *in order to receive what you want*, rather than as a practice of acknowledging all the blessings that are already flowing to them. This is usually unconscious, and it is a breakthrough for them when I make this distinction.

What exactly am I getting at here? I would explain it this way: if you are practicing gratitude in order to get what you want, then you still believe that your plan is better than God's plan. You are still trying to tell the universe *exactly in what form* it must answer your prayers. This is a symptom of fear, and if you are still *being* fearful and unworthy, the universe has no choice but to reinforce these beliefs about yourself and the world.

The key is to accept yourself as you are now, and give thanks for all the good that is already in your life. From there, you can begin to trust yourself and the universe more and more, until the day when you leap out of bed in the morning filled with enthusiasm to create yourself anew once more.

Make Your Beliefs Work For You, Not Against You

You'll see it when you believe it.

— *Wayne W. Dyer*

You have heard that your thoughts create your reality, and I agree that this is true. However, it is not just any thoughts that determine your experience, it is the ones you think over and over again, and these are also known as *beliefs*.

When most people hear the word 'belief,' they think of a concept or ideal that someone holds to be true. This is an accurate description, but the beliefs that we are going to concern ourselves with in this section are your *unconscious* beliefs. If you are like most people, these are the ones most responsible for shaping your life, and they are also difficult to become aware of precisely because they are unconscious. Yet it is in becoming aware of them that you gain the power to change them, if you find they are not serving you. It is one of my responsibilities as your coach to help you make your beliefs work for you, and it is one that I take very seriously indeed.

Why? Recall what I said in an earlier chapter: if you do not experience yourself as the creator of your life, it is because the vast majority of your choices are currently unconscious. These unconscious choices are, in turn, governed by unconscious beliefs that you formed as a child in response to your environment.

How exactly does this happen? Here is an example to illustrate:

Let's say your mother asks you to sweep the kitchen and you do, only to have her do it all over again to get it 'to her standards.' Whether she says this out loud or not is immaterial, for children learn primarily from what their parents do, not what they say. This pattern repeats itself between you and your mother in myriad ways as you grow up, and the message you receive is "I'll never be good enough, so why bother?" As a result you are unable to get and stay organized, leaving you prone to missing bill payments, etc.

Note that you may not ever consciously think to yourself "I am not good enough," but this thought has nevertheless coloured the uncountable small choices you have made, which created your life in its current form. In this case, the consequences might include a cluttered living environment, a lack of respect at work, a credit score damaged by missed payments, etc.

Let it be noted as well that your mother already believed that she herself was in some way not good enough, and it manifested as perfectionism or the tendency to criticise; she has simply passed it on to you, as all parents do. But it only affects you now because at some point, *you took it on*, and you continue to carry it today! The question is, why?

This is quite a normal experience, something we all do as part of our learning here on Earth. The problem arises when you carry a limiting belief like this far beyond the point when it is useful to you, allowing it to shape your life much longer than necessary. We do this because in our culture we are taught to believe that our thoughts are true, a fallacy that causes suffering in countless forms. If we were instead given tools and training to assist us in what I like to call 'mental and emotional hygiene,' I am quite sure the world we live in would look very different indeed.

Here is the point I really wish to drive home: if you can realize that your thoughts are not necessarily true, you can gain the freedom to choose the ones that support your highest goals and intentions, and *discard the ones that do not*. Since freedom of choice is universal law, the ability to do this is perhaps the one thing with the most power to 'open doors where there were only walls.'

So, are you ready to give it a go? I find that forgiveness work is often necessary before some people can embrace the (very liberating!) idea that their prison is entirely of their own making. Just remember that, even if a limiting belief might have at one time been necessary to your survival within your family, *no one is forcing you to keep it now*. You simply need permission, guidance and tools to access another way, and it is my intention as your coach to provide you with just that.

As I've said, the only person whose permission you *really* need to change your life is you, so if you find yourself resisting these ideas then I encourage you to revisit the forgiveness exercises that I have already shared. Otherwise, get out your journal and play with use the following questions as prompts to uncover your limiting beliefs:

- Ask your subconscious mind to show you three memories from your childhood that were central to the creation of your current belief system, and write them down briefly. Then look for what they have in common, and distil your core limiting beliefs from this information. You may wish to write to release immediately after this, if the memories are particularly charged.

- Playing 'devil's advocate,' write about why you believe you *cannot* have what you want. Intend that doing this will allow you to gain some distance from the unconscious beliefs that have run your life thus far. Write down the limiting beliefs you become aware of and create affirmations that counteract them, remembering to write them in positive form. Say these affirmations multiple times each day.

- After you have been practicing the exercises above daily for at least one week, take a quiet moment to journal on the following prompt: 'If I had absolutely no limits (time, money, etc.), what would I create?'

Journal on this topic for at least 15 minutes, longer if possible. It will be valuable to keep what you write handy, perhaps even typing it and printing it to post in a place where you will be able to view it often. If you are able to distil concrete goals from what you write, that is even better.

The work I do with my clients using the One Command™ Process is one of the most rewarding aspects of my practice, because it is where I often see real change happen very quickly. I hope that this will be only the start of your efforts at mental and emotional hygiene, and that you will consider taking this work deeper in the company of a qualified coach who can help you transform safely and in the way that best suits you. Above all, remember that you more than anyone have the right to be the author of your own life! I will end this chapter with a quote from Viktor Frankl that has inspired me for many years:

Everything can be taken from a man but one thing: the last of the human freedoms—to choose one's attitude in any given set of circumstances, to choose one's own way.

CHAPTER FIVE

Place Your Purpose at the Centre of Your Life

Remember that wherever your heart is, there you will find your treasure.

— Paulo Coelho, The Alchemist

B y now, you understand that the key to living a life of joy, purpose and passion is to re-awaken the power of your heart, because it is your passion that will lead you to your purpose. You know that you have the power to heal, and that when you align your will with the will of the Universe there is nothing that can stop what you seek from finding you. You have even learned how to uncover the limiting beliefs you took on as a child, and replace them with beliefs that support you in living your highest and best life.

What remains now is to integrate what you have learned into the daily rhythms of your life, in recognition that it is the choices you make in each moment that determine the shape your life takes overall. Most of all, it is your choice of who to be in each moment that determines your experience of life. Is it your intention to be grateful, peaceful and connected to something greater, or will you allow bitterness, self-criticism, or hopelessness to colour your choices? Above all, remember that you always have the power to choose.

What we are going to do in this chapter is explore what it will take to really put your joy, purpose and passion at the centre of your life. One of the best things about discovering your life's purpose is that it can serve as a compass for every choice you make, and will thus lead you to success as you define it. In fact, my personal definition of success is *you living your purpose and me living mine.* Since my purpose is to enable people to develop themselves to be their best and achieve their highest potential, and I am doing that through this book among other things, we are already halfway there! All that remains is for you to achieve the same, and we'll both have reached our goal.

Make Sure You Serve Your Self First

Service will come naturally, as part of who we are, when we allow ourselves to truly express our authenticity from the centre of our being.

— Anita Moorjani

At this point, you may have already drafted some possible statements of your life's purpose, and maybe you have even arrived at one that resonates strongly for you. If this is the case, I congratulate you! I also want to ask you a question: when you read your statement of your life's purpose, does it feel as though it serves yourself *first*? Really sit with this question and answer it honestly. If there is any part of your statement that does not *fully* resonate with your heart—that may have come from outside influences or is in any way associated with sacrifice for its own sake—I encourage you to continue refining it until that is no longer the case. Remember that a written statement is just a pointer to your purpose as you currently understand it; you should expect it to evolve as you do, and revise it periodically as needed.

I would like to share here a longer version of the quote that I began this section with. If you have not heard of author Anita Moorjani, I highly recommend both her first book, called *Dying to Be Me* and her second, which came out just last year and is called *What If This Is Heaven?* The first book is Anita's memoir of her four-year battle with lymphoma, which culminated in a Near-Death Experience (NDE) in which Anita experienced the truth of who she was beyond her body and received profound wisdom that she now shares with the world. She also fully healed from end-stage cancer, an outcome that Anita says she chose while in the NDE realm, but that science remains unable to explain. The second book is an exploration of how in large part, it is our cultural myths that prevent us from experiencing Heaven on Earth, and this quote is from that book. In its longer form, it reads as follows:

Service will come naturally, as part of who we are, when we allow ourselves to truly express our authenticity from the centre of our being. At one time, I used to give service because I felt I 'should' and because it was the 'right' thing to do. That kind of service comes from the head, not from the heart. It comes from a feeling of obligation or a sense of duty, and it can drain our energy if we keep bowing to the pressure of continuing to serve in this way. We think we're doing good, but it doesn't occur to us that to perform a service out of obligation is dishonest both to the receiver and to the giver...True service comes from the heart, and it comes naturally to us when we allow ourselves to just be who we really are...That's when we start to be of service, instead of performing a service. At that point, service stops being a heavy burden. Instead it becomes light and fun, and it then becomes a joy that uplifts us as well as the people who benefit.

We have discussed the fact that your true calling will usually involve serving others in some way, whether by designing and selling beautiful, socially-responsible consumer goods as a conscious entrepreneur, or by guiding others to love and truth as a teacher, minister or healer. Yet what I have found is that oftentimes, people have ideas about what service means that are not actually true for them. The fact is that even how you define service can be subject to limiting beliefs, and when that is the case your will find that the ways you choose to serve do not actually result in more joy and passion in your life. And what, I ask, is the point of that?

This is why I always make sure that my clients arrive at their purpose via their passions—because this is the best way I know to ensure that the purpose they uncover is in fact their *true* purpose, in which they serve their highest Self *at the same time that they serve others*. This is important because, as I mentioned earlier, you cannot give away to others what you do not have yourself. And in most cases, you are the one who must give to yourself first, and this then allows the universe to give to you in many forms.

I also wish to make a point here about the pitfalls of comparison. It is natural to compare yourself to those you admire who seem to have what it is you want, especially as you embark on a programme of self-transformation. While it is true that we can glean valuable information from observing others whose paths seem similar to our own, you must remember two things:

1. Regardless of outward appearance, you can never know for sure that someone is happy unless you ask them directly, and even then they may not answer honestly. Have you ever idealized someone, only to later be shocked by news of that person's marital problems or substance abuse? This holds as true for neighbours and co-workers as it does for celebrities. For some people, material success is more a source of misery than fulfilment—this may be their destiny, but I assure you that it does not have to be yours!

2. No matter how great the legacy or impact may be of someone you idealise, that does not mean that

Divine Will dictates you should serve in the same way they do. Remember that as a child of God, you are completely unique: there never has been, and never will be, anyone else exactly like you who can contribute in exactly the way that you can. Find that purpose and fulfil it, and you will be living your greatest destiny regardless of the opinions of others.

Indeed, the scale at which you serve does not even matter, for it is only the ego that puts stock in this. To the Creator and your soul, there is no difference between someone whose highest purpose is to be a good wife and mother and the great teachers and change-makers of history, for all are part of one indivisible whole. What matters is that you live in accordance with your own unique truth as much of the time as possible, and only you can know when you are doing that.

The point is that you must never allow comparison of yourself with someone else to reinforce the belief that you are somehow not good enough. As far as I can tell, this belief is shared by 90% or more of humanity, though it manifests in many forms. It is so important to commit yourself to releasing this belief one layer at a time, for it is this more than anything that prevents you from trusting yourself.

In case you hadn't noticed, both of the points I make above are about trusting yourself. While a skilled coach and other helpers will be great assets on your path of transformation, you must always remember that you are the ultimate authority on your own truth. The minute you feel that someone you look up to is trying to tell you your truth, you must realise that that relationship may be nearing the end of its useful life. If you can trust yourself and your Creator enough to let such relationships go in favour of your truth, then you can know that great things are coming to you.

Let Go Of What No Longer Serves

I believe that everything happens for a reason. People change so that you can learn to let go, things go wrong so that you appreciate them when they're right, you believe lies so you eventually learn to trust no one but yourself, and sometimes good things fall apart so better things can fall together.

— *Marilyn Monroe*

Now we are ready to address one of the greatest questions that my clients and I ask as the momentum of transformation builds: what if a point comes when you realise that some of your relationships no longer serve your highest good? Will you have the courage to allow them to shrink or drop away, even if you do not know what will come in their place?

Anita Moorjani also has some profound wisdom to share on this front. She returned from her NDE profoundly changed, with what might be called her 'false self' having completely dropped away. As she healed and attempted to resume a normal life, she found that she no longer had much in common with many of the people she had associated with prior to the NDE.

You could say she was fortunate in that her closest relationships, such as those with her husband, her mother and her brother grew even stronger after her experience. Yet she still struggled for a time with the fact that some of the people she had previously considered friends did not seem to have any interest in her authentic self. Since it was no longer possible for her to be someone she wasn't however, she simply allowed these relationships to dissolve, knowing that new people who *were* interested in her true self would come along to replace them. And that is exactly what happened!

Not only did Anita find new friends who were as excited about the truths she had experienced as she was, her story miraculously found its way into the hands of mega-author Wayne Dyer, who himself became a dear friend and mentor and was instrumental in the publication of her first book. The rest, as they say, is history, and it is continuing to unfold in miraculous ways.

I would argue that it was Anita's newfound determination to live her truth, and the complete banishment of self-doubt that resulted from her NDE, that allowed a life beyond imagining to unfold for her. In just 10 years, she went from an unremarkable career as a cross-cultural consultant, to the edge of death, to a global career as an inspirational speaker and author. She attributes all of it to the resolve she had upon her return to physical life to love herself unconditionally and to never again deny who she was in response to the opinions of others. She also knew that she would not have to *do* anything specific to make the destiny that awaited her happen—that it would all unfold miraculously simply as a result of her being her true self.

I admit that hers is an extraordinary story, but it certainly reinforces the idea that anything is possible when we align with our true selves. I wish to return again to the idea I shared earlier that the unknown is the source of at least as many pleasant surprises as it is unpleasant ones, and which type of experience you see more of is largely determined by your dominant belief system. As Wayne Dyer liked to say, 'you'll see it when you believe it!'

In the NDE realm Anita Moorjani encountered her late father, who encouraged her to 'go back and live your life fearlessly!' So here are some questions to ask yourself at this stage:

- Are there relationships in your life that you know do not support you in letting your light shine? If so, ask yourself how you can begin to give to yourself the things that you have looked to these relationships for in the past. How can you let go of what prevents you from being the love that you are, and fan the divine spark within you into a robust flame? Remember, most fear is illusory, and if you are not experiencing the love that you are you will do well to practice self-love and address fear on an on-going basis.

- Where can you find a community whose values match your own? How can you spend more time with people who share your passions? Just as the teacher appears when the student is ready, so too do wonderful allies emerge from the woodwork when you commit to living your truth. Imagine the qualities you'd like to see in a friend or associate, practice them yourself, and watch the magic happen!

- Who can you forgive, and where can you take responsibility—no matter how small—for each of your relationships? This is sometimes the hardest question to answer honestly, but it is vital to explore it if you really wish to be free. There is always some degree of complicity on the part of both parties when a relationship is out of balance. As Eleanor Roosevelt famously wrote, "no one can make you feel inferior without your consent."

Have the Courage to Be Who You Are

To be yourself in a world that is constantly trying to make you something else is the greatest accomplishment.

— Ralph Waldo Emerson

Here is a powerful secret: while some of our relationships may cause us suffering, they can only do so to the extent that we *buy into the false self-concepts they perpetuate.* This means that when you really find the courage to be your authentic self—to *live your life fearlessly*—your relationships will come into balance on their own. Can you imagine what that would look like?

To return to the example from an earlier chapter, suppose your relationship with your mother has always been rife with criticism. Let us say you call your mother to tell her about something important to you, and she belittles it, leaving you resentful. You hang up the phone feeling put out not only with her, but with the world: thoughts such as "why do I bother when I'll never be good enough" and "she has no right to say those things to me" wreak havoc on your peace of mind. What your mother said only reflects her perceptions, not your truth, yet you are allowing it to affect you! This is a recipe for suffering.

What do you suppose would happen if you simply stopped buying into that story? It may sound like an abstract question, but a story from one of my clients paints a very concrete picture of what is possible:

This client was one of those people who just always felt different. She was the only child of a well-off, secular family that valued intelligence, hard work and education above all else. As a child however, she saw, heard and sensed things that she was not supposed to know, for while she was intelligent enough, she was also profoundly intuitive.

Fear of rejection caused her to shut her abilities down very early, but worse than that, she essentially rejected *herself* at a young age, concluding that if she was so very different from everyone around her then there must be something wrong with her. It must be so, for how could the whole world be mad and only she saw things as they really were? But we must ask ourselves how many people could tell a comparable story, or how many would call the world we live in mad to one degree or another.

As you might imagine, this caused my client no small amount of suffering in her early years. While she knew that her parents loved her in their way, she did not feel understood by them at all, and she was bullied badly at school. She thus entered young adulthood nearly friendless and with life goals that had nothing to do with her authentic self, because she simply could not allow herself to know who she really was. Somehow her subconscious mind had decided that self-expression was dangerous, and this belief was so strong she could not overcome it on her own.

Despite finding moderate success as a result of her privileged upbringing and good education, this client could never shake the feeling that something was profoundly missing from her life. Then, through a series of serendipitous events in her mid-twenties, she became involved with an organisation that taught intuitive skills and spiritual healing techniques through weekly classes. That was the point when things really began to shift for her.

My client was compelled to continue attending these classes even though her logical mind could make no sense of what she did there. She continued to attend once a week for many years, slowly building trust in her powerful intuitive and self-healing abilities and giving herself permission to *be* her true self for the first time she could remember. In her work with me, she also did a great deal of self-love and forgiveness work that led to the healing of some of the core wounds that she had taken on as a child.

My client now makes a good living as an intuitive coach, sharing her passion for spirit and teaching in service of her clients' growth. What's more, her relationship with her parents has become much more loving and relaxed, even thought they still don't begin to understand her! Because she is being true to herself, her parents are free to be themselves as well—each person is allowed his or her own reality, and their relationships reflect their spiritual contracts rather than the old, painful ego patterns. The nature of the relationship changed, but in this case it was able to continue in another form. It took bravery for my client to heal her deepest wounds, but when she did it turned out to be a win-win for everyone.

This client once showed me a collection of greeting cards that she had received from her mother over the years. Each one had come from a store near her mother's home, and was not remarkable on its own. Yet my client found a sense of profound recognition in the message each contained, as if her mother's hand had been guided to choose each card in affirmation of the beauty of my clients' light, beyond the role of daughter. My client keeps these cards close at hand, and revisits them when she needs to rekindle her faith in her choice to follow her highest path.

Once again, I'll end this chapter with a quote that I feel encapsulates its core message, this time from the great Sufi poet Hafiz:

I wish I could show you, when you are lonely or in darkness, the astonishing light of your own being

CHAPTER SIX

Commit to Your Purpose Now

I've finally stopped running away from myself. Who else is there better to be?

— Goldie Hawn

You are now more than halfway through this book—how are you feeling? As you have no doubt understood by now, it takes courage to discover your purpose because it sometimes means changing aspects of your life that do not currently allow you to express it. If you are like many people, you may fear learning that you are in the wrong position or even career, and being faced with the monumental task of overhauling your life as a result.

This fear may be one of the biggest reasons why more people do not engage in the self-exploration required to discover and live their purpose. This is most unfortunate because remember, fear is False Evidence Appearing Real, and it results from a limited point of view caused by limiting beliefs that are within your power to change. What is more, as author Bronnie Ware shares in her book *The Top Five Regrets of the Dying: A Life Transformed by the Dearly Departing*, literally the number one regret that she heard from dying patients in eight years spent as a palliative care nurse was, "I wish I'd had the courage to live a life true to myself, not the life others expected of me."

I have said it before and I will say it again: if you are reading this, you already have what it takes to live your purpose and achieve your dreams. That said, like all of us you can benefit from qualified support in your efforts to reach your full potential, and it is my life's purpose to provide you with just that.

Fly High, Land Safely

Transferring your passion to your job is far easier than finding a job that happens to match your passion.

— Seth Godin in Linchpin: Are You Indispensable?

If you fear that aligning your life with your highest purpose will require too much change, let me assure you that this is very seldom the case. I have worked with many people who have chosen to embark on the path of purpose, and I have written on the steps required for a successful career transition in my book *Fly High, Land Safely: The Ultimate Guide to Career Transition for Executives*.

In my work as an executive coach and consultant, I address the concerns surrounding this topic in two ways:

First, it has been my observation that for many people, creating a career that better reflects their life purpose does not require a major break with the past—indeed, it is surprising how often relatively minor adjustments in role or focus can make a huge difference.

Secondly, I remind my clients that ignoring the disparity between their inner purpose and outer life won't make it go away; rather, suppressing the truth once you have seen it tends to snowball into much more disruptive consequences than you would have experienced had you embraced change earlier. If a disparity does become apparent, the key is to ask for, seek out, and prioritise receiving help from mentors and other advisors who can help you with the transition. It is important to remember that you are never alone.

Perhaps best of all, identifying your purpose for being on the planet takes the guesswork out of making important life decisions. As you combine what you love to do with what you want to accomplish in the world, you begin to comprehend what you are supposed to be doing with your life. Discovering your purpose takes the guesswork out of living, which can save you a lot of frustration, money, headaches, heartaches and time.

As your consciousness coach, I *know* that it is possible for you to align your life with your soul's purpose and that when you do, you will be rewarded in ways you cannot currently imagine. With patience, perseverance, and lightness, you can fly high, land safely, and never look back.

Spend Your Life Doing What Matters

Our greatest fear should not be of failure, but of succeeding at things in life that don't really matter.

— Pastor Francis Chan

On the subject of looking back, I want to return for a moment to Bronnie Ware's work. Ms. Ware spent eight years as a palliative care nurse in Australia, and she published her deeply personal memoir of that work in 2011 in response to the many requests she received to do so. The copy I keep on my bookshelf is dog-eared and worn because I have found that, despite the distaste with which most people view the topic of death in our culture, when you really want to get to the truth there is no better teacher. I believe that St. Francis of Assisi was speaking to this when he composed the final stanza of his world-famous prayer:

For it is in giving that we receive
It is in pardoning that we are pardoned
It is in dying, that we are born
Into Eternal Life.

What do you suppose he means by those last two lines? I have mused upon their meaning for many years, and I have concluded that these lines refer to the state of purpose, passion and joy that can only be yours when you fully align your will with the Divine will for your life. I once saw a bumper sticker that stated this truth another way and made me laugh too: "If you can't find God, you moved." I say again that the Divine spark is within you, but to experience its bliss you have to be willing to walk through the fire.

Let me take a moment here to ask you a question that has the potential to profoundly change your life if you will let it: who is it, precisely, that dies with your body? Is it the part of you that created your Purpose, the one that is always at one with your Creator? Of course not, because that part of you is eternal; it has intentions and it observes the events of your life, but it is not actually born and cannot actually die. Who is it, then, that ceases to exist with your last breath, and what if that persona is less real than the higher part of you that knows why you are here?

The answer of course is your ego, or personality. This is the part of you that identifies with your body and mind and fears death, but if you really wish to commit to a life of purpose you must be willing to allow its role to diminish. This is the part of you that perpetuates your fears and expends a great deal of energy worrying, trying to please others, etc. It certainly serves a purpose in that it allows you to function in this reality, but it should be relegated to the passenger seat rather than the driver's seat in the vehicle of your life. Otherwise you will arrive at a destination very different from the one you were aiming at when you first chose to come into this life, and while I believe we can come back as many times as we please—that is, you can never really get it wrong—why not shoot for the moon?

No one wants to get to the end of their life and realise that they spent most of their precious time on Earth living a lie. But because our culture is so intent on perpetuating untruth, it takes real courage and a strong commitment to growth to let the lies drop away. Can you find within your heart enough faith to believe that if you are willing to let go of your false self, your true self will emerge dazzling in its beauty? It is certainly a leap of faith, for the ego believes only what it can perceive through the five senses. Yet I know that this light exists in you, and that you will regret it at the end of your life if you do not at least attempt to live in alignment with it.

On that note and without further ado, here is the complete list of Top Five Regrets of the Dying, according to Bronnie Ware:

1. *I wish I'd had the courage to live a life true to myself, not the life others expected of me.*

This was by far the most common regret Ms. Ware encountered, especially among the women she cared for who had for the most part lived within traditional homemaker roles. Another way to say it might be, 'I wish I had made more time for my dreams and aspirations'—in other words, your purpose.

I want you to take a moment now to stroke your face and repeat these words:

"My life depends on my living my purpose."

If I have not convinced you of that by now, I hope you will heed the warning offered by those for whom it was too late.

2. *I wish I hadn't worked so hard.*

In contrast to the first regret, this one was most prevalent among men. Many had spent the vast majority of their time and energy fulfilling the breadwinner role and wished they had spent more quality time with family and friends.

3. *I wish I'd had the courage to express my feelings.*

This regret was more evenly distributed with regard to gender than the first two, but Ms. Ware feels this is one area that has improved a great deal with younger generations, who feel a much greater freedom to express themselves than their parents and grandparents did due to the increased availability of therapy and other tools for self-improvement.

4. *I wish I had stayed in touch with my friends.*

Many people in their final days are struck with a strong desire to re-connect with friends and family that they were once close to. It may surprise you to hear that this is one of the top five regrets of the dying, but I believe it because I have seen the power that quality relationships have to improve people's experience of life both personally and professionally. There is no question that maintaining quality relationships takes work, but this regret suggests that the rewards will be worth it when it matters most.

I also want to add that while staying in touch on social media is great, you still need to make sure you are taking the time to really enjoy and share life with those closest to you, unplugged and *in person*. Prior generations did not have social media, but there is some evidence that they experienced a sense of isolation less frequently than we do today. So make sure that you do not allow the lure of technology to distract you from the kinds of quality interactions that you will look back on fondly later in life.

5.   *I wish I had let myself be happier.*

Surprise! Happiness is a choice! But of course by now you knew that... right? The bad news is that if you are like most people, you have a happiness set-point; that is, there is a level of happiness you are comfortable with that it is difficult to let yourself surpass. This is most often due to limiting beliefs such as 'nothing good lasts' (neither does anything 'bad,' but never mind that), or 'if I am too happy I will tempt Fate' (as if God has nothing better to do than smite poor souls who dare to stop being victims and choose happiness).

Think about it, and be honest—has there ever been a time when you were feeling extra good, and then something happened to 'bring you down' and you almost felt relieved? Again, if you are like many people, you may have taken these events as 'proof' that your limiting beliefs are true, but I say again that *you see what you believe*. What happened was evidence, all right, but not for the truth of the belief, simply of the belief's presence in your mind.

You are not your beliefs, so why do you hold onto these patterns that no longer serve you? Only you can answer this question, and only you can take the steps necessary to change. Just remember as you do so that help is always available when you need it—you have only to ask, and the universe will provide. As your consciousness coach, I am able to guide you thorough 6 Steps in The One Command™ to remove disempowering beliefs and replace them with what you want instead.

The good news is that it is possible to 'raise your set point' with some very simple practices, especially those involving mindfulness and gratitude. I have already shared several such practices in this book, so my question to you is, have you been engaging with them each day? If not, what is your excuse? Are you now willing to do away with excuses *this instant*, and commit to living your purpose once and for all?

If the answer is 'yes,' then please keep reading and let us work together. If it is 'no,' you should accept that as your honest answer and return to this book when the time feels right to you. As I have said, in the long run you cannot get it wrong, and it will not serve you to pursue this path if you cannot fully choose it at this time. For as Vietnamese Buddhist monk, teacher and author Thich Nhat Hanh says so eloquently:

There is no way to happiness. Happiness is the way.

If you really want to reap the benefits that this book is offering you, please do not let another day go by without doing something to align your life more fully with your joy, even if it is something small. The choice is always yours—do not listen to any voice that says otherwise, *especially* if it is in your own head!

Make Today The Day Your Life Changes

There are two great days in a person's life: the day we are born and the day we discover why.

— *William Barclay*

Purpose tells you why your life is worth living, and helps you define your values. In his book *The Power of Purpose*, Richard Leider asked a cross-section of adults over age sixty-five this question: "If you could live your life over again, what would you do differently?" Three themes emerged from the replies, and it is interesting how closely they parallel the themes that Bronnie Ware uncovered in her survey of the dying. The respondents said they would:

1.   Be more reflective,
2.   Be more courageous, and
3.   Be clear earlier about their purpose.

In a way, you could say that the first two themes both relate to the third, which is the main subject of this book. It takes courage to explore your purpose for reasons we have already discussed, and you cannot know why you are here without a commitment to reflection either. It is only when you choose these two qualities—reflection and courage—that your purpose becomes available to you, and that is the key to everything. In my unique *Beacon's Leadership Star System*™, there is a subsystem *The Leader's Code*™, which starts with courage because this is one of the most important virtues of a great leader.

Other researchers have reached similar conclusions. In a 2002 study, Ron and Suzan Krannich found that 50% of Americans said they would make a different career choice today than they made when they first entered the job market. They were not necessarily unhappy with their current work, but perceived that they might have been happier had they made different career choices when they were young and inexperienced. I maintain that it is preferable to embrace a certain amount of risk in pursuit of a life and career that fulfils you, rather than continue doing work that leaves you feeling drained each day in pursuit of safety. If you sacrifice being happy now thinking that you will do what you love when you retire, it is possible that that chance may never come, for none of us knows how much time we will be given on this Earth. That, to me, seems like a far greater risk.

> *And most important, have the courage to follow your heart and intuition. They somehow already know what you truly want to become. Everything else is secondary.*
> — Steve Jobs, Stanford commencement speech, June 2005

Another study by Marty Nemko and Paul and Sarah Edwards in 1998 revealed that more than 46% of men and 40% of women say they are still trying to figure out the meaning and purpose of their life. In his book *How to Figure Out, Once And For All, What You Really Want to Do With Your Life,* author Darrel Daybre observes that:

> *From the time we are born, we are on a search to discover our life purpose. Most people never do find it. Yet there is a void, an emptiness until we discover our purpose in life.*

As we discussed in chapter three, the path to discovering your life purpose begins with noticing what captivates you and opens your heart. Once you begin to look, you will see that these things run like a golden thread through your life, weaving your destiny into a tapestry of breath-taking beauty.

You were taught early in life to focus on what you would do and become when you reached adulthood. As you become aware your life purpose, you can begin to give attention to what you wish to take away from this life, and how you wish to be remembered. You can begin to articulate what it is you came here to experience, learn and understand. Yet, you can only get there by taking a step *now*, so the question is, what will that step be for you? If you sit in silence and ask sincerely, your inner wisdom may just come through with an answer.

A New Way to Think About Power

*Always say 'yes' to the present moment... Surrender to
what is. Say 'yes' to life - and see how life starts suddenly
working for you rather than against you.*

— Eckhart Tolle

Each time you sit with the questions that I ask you in
these pages, each time you put pen to paper in pursuit of your
highest truth, you are that much closer to the life of your
dreams. I find that with many of my clients, a turning point
comes when they realise that the rewards of a life of purpose
far exceed the hard work it can sometimes take to get there. If
you are feeling concerned at the prospect of making
'sacrifices' in pursuit of your joy, purpose and passion, I hope
that what I am about to tell you will help you put those
concerns to rest once and for all.

First, recall that your limiting beliefs only have as much
power as you give them. When you are able to free yourself
from these self-imposed limitations, you begin to grasp that
true power comes with surrender to a higher calling, and
miracles become possible for you. In his phenomenal book
The 8th Habit, which expands on the ideas he outlines in *The 7
Habits of Highly Effective People*, Stephen R. Covey speaks of
'sacrificing something good for something better.' He sees the
willingness to undertake this type of sacrifice as the main
difference between people who do great things and those who
don't. The challenge, of course, is to trust your inner knowing

that the time has indeed come to let go, and I believe this is why Goethe said, "As soon as you trust yourself, you will know how to live." This is what I mean when I speak of surrender, and I hope you will embrace this distinction for when you do, it will change your life.

The old narrative of 'power over' implores us to out-smart and out-compete others, with their 'surrender' as the hallmark of our victory. This kind of power is easily observable in the animal kingdom where males in many species fight for dominance to ensure that their genes are passed on. This patriarchal model of power is still all too prevalent in human organisations, but for some years now we have seen a more inclusive, collaborative leadership model begin to take hold. These models aim to allow each voice to be heard, creating a safe space for people to speak their truth even when they know that others may disagree.

What does this have to do with the kind of surrender I am talking about, and what does it have to do with purpose? One of the things required to live on purpose is integrity, and this means speaking your truth and trusting that it will bring you where you need to go. How many times have you quashed your truth out of fear that others would react negatively, or even denied it to yourself because of your limiting beliefs? When you do this you sabotage yourself, but you emerge victorious when you surrender your destructive patterns and ask that the spaces the destructive patterns leave behind be filled with light. In this case, *it is not your true self that you are surrendering, but the false self that prevents you from actualizing our dreams.*

Surrendering to the greatness that the Universe has planned for you takes courage, and it is also one of the fastest ways to arrive at a life lived on purpose. All you have to do is take the first step and ask the Universe to lead you, and it will do so, a step at a time.

CHAPTER SEVEN

Your Purpose Gives You Clarity and Power

We must look for ways to be an active force in our own lives. We must take charge of our own destinies, design a life of substance and truly begin to live our dreams.

— Les Brown

Throughout this book I have been emphasising the link between your purpose, your passion, and your joy. At the end of the last chapter, I also began to explore the topic of power, and how true empowerment may look very different from how you have thought of power thus far. I believe that we only arrive at true power when we finally understand that our greatest power lies within, in our intentions and our ability to choose how we respond to each situation that life sends our way. This chapter is about how knowing your purpose enhances your ability to do that.

In my coaching work over the years, I have developed a conceptual framework that I call the Six Powers of Purpose. I use this framework to help my clients understand why it is so important for them to know why they are here, and to put this knowledge to good use. In this chapter we will discuss the six powers of purpose in detail, and how each contributes to your clarity and power. I encourage you to revisit this chapter frequently so that you can fully absorb what is available to you here. You may wish to reserve a couple of pages in your journal for each Power to jot down notes about them as you are inspired to.

If I have not already convinced you of the importance of discovering and living your life's purpose, I hope to do so now once and for all. I hope you will stay with me until the end, so that you may gain maximum benefit from the time we have spent together on these pages thus far. Enjoy reading about the Six Powers of Purpose, and make note of any questions you may have about them so we can discuss them should we ever have the opportunity to work together. I appreciate your commitment to becoming who are meant to be.

The Power of Who You Are

Who you are speaks so loudly I cannot hear what you are saying.

— Ralph Waldo Emerson

By this point in the book, you should understand why this power is first on the list. As we have discussed, your beliefs create your thoughts and therefore your experience of reality, and underneath it all is the quality of *who you are being*. To me, the quote from Emerson suggests that it is this subtle quality is in fact much more powerful than the specific words you said. Why? Just think about it for a moment: there are so many words and phrases where meaning can change completely depending on the intention with which they are said. The same is true of actions, of course; very often it is the intention behind an action, far more than the action itself, that is most significant.

There are endless examples I could give, but I want you to think up a few of your own and write them in your journal: have you ever experienced a dissonance between either words or actions and the intention behind them—either in yourself or in another—and how did you react to that? Next, think about a time when you or another person spoke or acted in complete integrity, and the impression that made. Just taking a moment to focus on these things reveals the power of who you are being—that is, your *intention*—beyond the shadow of a doubt.

Some teachers and authors shy away from discussing this topic because it is difficult to measure, but the difference between those authors and me is that I am not trying to tell you your truth, I am rather pointing you to a truth that only you can know. Who you are being is indeed 'un-definable' in the sense that it cannot always be labelled by the conscious mind, but this is not the same as being un-knowable. When you realise this and begin to pay attention firstly, to your inner state, you will soon observe a correlation between your state of being on any given day and how you experience your life that day. Then you will be the master of your thoughts and feelings instead of the other way around, and you will be amazed at the things that start to happen for you.

I know that what will change your life more than anything, is to become aware of the myriad small choices you make in each moment, about who you desire to be as you navigate the currents of life, and that the key to a life of joy, purpose and passion is to bring greater awareness to all of these choices. You are at your most powerful when who you are being is in alignment with your Purpose.

In fact, I would go so far as to say that when you fully commit to the purpose that resonates with your soul, literally anything becomes possible for you because you are then aligning your will with Divine will. If you feel overwhelmed with all that you have to do, remember that Mahatma Gandhi led a peaceful revolution in India, yet he spent the first half of each day in silence! Because Gandhi was so fully in integrity with his purpose, the actions he did take were many times more powerful than they would have otherwise been, and he therefore *accomplished more by doing less.* As he wisely observed, "Happiness is when what you think, what you say, and what you do are in harmony." This is the power of who you are being.

The Power of Who You Will Become

Don't let who you were talk you out of who you are becoming.

— Bob Goff

This power relates to the first power in the sense that it refers to who you aim to be in the future. Do you remember a few chapters back, when I introduced the idea that in order to have something, you must become who you would need to be to have it? This is the power of who you will become.

Remember that what you seek is seeking you; if you do not now have something you deeply desire, whether tangible or intangible, then there is some way in which you are not allowing it to manifest in your life. If you feel any internal resistance when you imagine actually having that which you seek, this indicates that you have limiting beliefs that are preventing you from accepting the gifts the universe is trying to give you. That is what I am pointing to with this power.

I would add to the quote above that you must not let *who you are right now* talk you out of who you are becoming, either. This is where the delicate dance between acceptance and striving comes in: you must explore the ways in which you currently resist who you would need to be to have your dreams, which are rooted in your limiting beliefs, and take steps to change without blaming yourself in any way. While it is certainly not impossible to make progress on your own in this area, I can tell you for sure that it will go much, much faster if you are receiving qualified support with an experienced coach.

The Power of Your Capacity

Strength does not come from physical capacity. It comes from an indomitable will.

— Mahatma Gandhi

When you are in full integrity with your Purpose, your capacity expands in every way. Not only do you become better able to 'work smarter, not harder,' you also may find things happening for you in what might be called a miraculous way. This may sound like a fringe idea, but I have seen it happen with my clients many times and I can testify this to be true in my own life. As soon as you commit fully to your purpose, support for your goals emerges seemingly out of the blue, and you find that you are making more progress in a week than you did in a month previously.

Commitment is so central to living a life on purpose. Heed these words.

Until one is committed, there is hesitancy, the chance to draw back, always ineffectiveness. Concerning all acts of initiative (and creation), there is one elementary truth, the ignorance of which kills countless ideas and splendid plans: that the moment one definitely commits oneself, then Providence moves too. All sorts of things occur to help one that would never otherwise have occurred. A whole stream of events issues from the decision, raising in one's favour all manner of unforeseen incidents and meetings and material assistance, which no man could have dreamt would have come his way. Whatever you can do, or dream you can, begin it. Boldness has genius, power, and magic in it!

— William Hutchinson Murray

This is what I refer to as the process of co-creation, and it is about aligning your actions and intentions with the timing of the universe. Here is what it looks like:

Let us say you are an entrepreneur and you are truly passionate about your ideas, but you have been pursuing them outside of your normal work hours while you wait for the breakthrough you need to go full-time. You have been straining your body and mind in pursuit of your passion, yet while all the pieces are in place there still seems to be something missing.

You set up a few coaching sessions with me in an effort to uncover the reasons why that breakthrough has not happened yet, and we dig up some limiting beliefs that are keeping you from it. I walk you through The One Command™ to clear your limiting beliefs. You commit to a daily practice of affirmation that is designed to reprogram your mind with beliefs that support your efforts instead of negating them, and after a month, you are contacted by an investor who happened on your product online and believes it could go big. This is the breakthrough you have been waiting for, a moment of grace that arrived in response to your new capacity to *have what you want*.

You released your limits, and your capacity became that of the universe itself as a result. You will still work hard, but it will not feel like work because you will be spending each day doing what you love. There is no better feeling than this.

The Power of Your Relationships

We make a living by what we get; we make a life by what we give.

— Winston Churchill

In the same way that committing to integrity with your Purpose will activate your Power of Capacity, bringing your highest and best self to all of your relationships will leverage their power to your advantage. As I have stated before, your Purpose is about giving more than it is about getting, and when you are living your highest truth you have so much more to give; indeed, giving itself becomes the greatest pleasure. It really is a win-win for all involved, because when you make everyone's life better, your life will automatically expand in positive and outstanding ways.

You may wish to delve deeper on the topic of relationship intelligence in my book *The Beacon Technique: 6 Conscious Blueprints to Experience Your Joy*. Among the nuggets within the book is a chapter on getting what you want with relationship intelligence including how to listen for possibilities and how to listen others into existence.

You may ask, what is the single most effective tool for enhancing relationships? If you are old enough to have spent much time with other people, you may already know it is communication. If you think that communication is mainly about talking however, then let me remind you of a phrase that you may have heard as a child: "We have two ears and only one mouth, so we should listen twice as much as we talk."

While there is no question that it is important to be able to express yourself with clarity and compassion, it is at least as important to cultivate good listening skills. We are all at different stages on the path of learning how to listen, and your experience of relationships will reflect that. It can take some work to learn how to hear what someone is really saying, versus what it is you *think* they are saying, which may be coloured by your own perceptions.

If you are thinking, 'this is nothing new to me, of course my relationships are sources of power in my life,' then let me ask you this: are you still waiting for others to give you permission to be your true self? Are you waiting for others to give you the love, respect, and confidence that you have as yet been unwilling or unable to bestow upon yourself?

If so, then let us clarify something very important: your relationship with yourself is the primary relationship in your life. If you thought that your primary relationship was with your spouse, this may feel jarring, but I assure you that if you already have a good relationship with your partner, then improving your relationship with yourself will only make it better. Conversely, if your most important relationships could benefit from some extra attention and intention, then your efforts to improve you relationship with yourself will bear fruit in that case as well.

Of course, you living your purpose, whether personal or professional, will improve all of the relationships in your life. That said, the person with the greatest influence on your experience of life is you, and when you have a positive relationship with yourself, all of your efforts to live your passion and purpose will be more effective. Focus your efforts on healing your relationship with yourself—especially with your inner child, mother and father—and you will be amazed by the ripple effects it creates in your life.

The Power of Your Spirituality

Life will give you whatever experience is most helpful for the evolution of your consciousness. How do you know this is the experience you need? Because this is the experience you are having at the moment.

— Eckhart Tolle, A New Earth: Awakening to Your
Life's Purpose

You have no doubt noticed that the theme of spirituality is woven throughout this book, and there is a very good reason for that. I am a firm believer in a higher power and in the kind of practical spirituality that can help you experience a sense of joy, purpose and passion each and every day. I certainly understand why people dislike dogma, and that is not what I am speaking of at all. Rather, I am speaking of something that for me has been a source of peace, joy and manifestation beyond all understanding: a spirituality of direct experience.

I bring the mind of a scientist to spirituality, in the sense that I will try anything for a week and observe the results in my life. Then I can pass those tools and techniques that I have found beneficial on to my clients and students, knowing that I have tested them in my own life first. I feel this helps me approach the subject of spirituality with integrity, and without excluding any particular belief system. So far, my clients agree.

Understand that I will never ask you to believe in anything, only to explore the possibility that forces beyond the reach of your five senses are at work in your life. If you are willing to do that, then you may very well find yourself having experiences like the one I describe below:

If you were with me in July 2013, you would have found yourself in the Bravo suite of the Verta Hotel (now the Crown Plaza), Battersea, London. I would have led you in a 3-day programme on Commanding Wealth™ with six other persons, three of whom were paying and three of whom were not. You would have seen me giving my all, leading you to the realm of your greatness in order to empower you to become healthy, wealthy, wise and free, to enable you to become aware of your abilities, to inspire you to lead with courage, authenticity, love, wisdom and through the Divine light of Spirit. That, after all, is why I am here!

There can be no doubt that leading this workshop was an expression of my purpose, but on the final day of the programme I began to question, is it worth it? It is amazing how doubt can still creep in, even when one is clearly aligned with one's purpose—but you will soon see why it is important not to listen to doubt! As I packed up to go home, you would have witnessed one of the paying clients saying to me, "Neslyn, I want to honour your dedication. I felt every word you uttered was directed to me, and your words spoke to my heart. I don't know why, but my inner voice tells me to cover your bill at the hotel in full for the three days, please allow me to do so."

You would have seen me graciously accepting this kind person's offer, while inwardly saying thank you to God for taking care of my needs. Not only had I delivered the programme in a comfortable and beautiful environment overlooking the river Thames, I had also been provided food and beverage as the client was covering the whole bill. I know this happened because it is not about me, it is about the service that I give in line with what I feel to be my Divine purpose. This is the power of your spirituality.

I have found that many spiritual truths can best be expressed in paradox, which can be defined as two contradicting truths that together point to one. One paradox that has been true for me is the following: that whenever you are living your passion, you will be tested. Things will show up to test how much you care, or you could say that the old self-defeating patterns you are letting go of have a life of their own, and are making a last-ditch effort to keep you in their clutches. Either way you feel fearful, so the question is how do you respond?

What I said earlier about beliefs holds true here as well: if fear shows up for you when you know you are living your purpose, you can be sure the fear is illusory; it is just the universe giving you another opportunity to choose faith. In those moments, you will experience doubt, which is the opposite of faith. The more consistently you are able to choose faith however, the less the fear will show up, until it is revealed for the illusion it is once and for all. Remember not to believe your fears, and you will be well on your way to living the power of your spirituality.

The Power of Concentration and Flow

When we choose a goal and invest ourselves in it to the limits of concentration, whatever we do will be enjoyable. And once we have tasted this joy, we will redouble our efforts to taste it again. This is the way the self grows.

— Mihaly Csikszentmihalyi, Flow: The Psychology of Optimal Experience

Your purpose keeps you aligned and focused on what matters; it allows you to become clear about what drives you and what gets you out of bed. When you are doing something you feel passionate about, time disappears and you can work long days without feeling depleted because you have released your resistance and jumped into the flow of creation.

Do you remember when I asked you to write down activities that make you lose track of time? When you are engaged in those activities, you are in a state of what might be called 'flow.' Mihaly Csikszentmihalyi, psychologist and author of the book Flow: The Psychology of Optimal Experience, defines Flow as a state of deep enjoyment, creativity, and a total involvement with life. When you are in that state you never want it to end, and if you can work at a career that gets you in the flow you will leap out of bed in the morning.

In my work with clients, I have found that what could be called the 'flow' mindset, like so many other things, is akin to a muscle that can be built with training. As the quote above suggests, sometimes it is the very act of investing yourself in a task 'to the limits of concentration' that ignites your passion. The activities that generate the most flow will vary from person to person, and they may change for you over time, but it is important to determine what they are so that you can hone your 'optimal experience' muscles. I highly recommend Dr. Csikszentmihalyi's book if you are interested in diving deeper into this subject.

Now that you are armed with knowledge of the six powers of purpose, it is time to really let the rubber meet the road. I look forward to helping you put all you have learned thus far into practice in the pages to come.

CHAPTER EIGHT

Claim Your Purpose and Passion Now

It is never too late to be what you might have been.

— George Eliot

By now, you have probably begun to wonder what next steps you can take to bring more joy, passion and purpose to your life, *starting today*. If so you're in luck, because that is exactly what we are going to be discussing in the rest of this book. If you are like me, you expect to be rewarded for the time you spend reading a book like this with practical tools and advice that you can apply immediately to improve your life. I do not take the gift of your time for granted, so that is precisely what I aim to provide. There are so many self-help books out there; my goal is for this to be one of the most worthwhile ones you ever read.

Of course, no matter what I fill these pages with, ultimately the choice rests with you to internalise what I share here and put it into regular practice in your daily life. I know that many of you reading this will derive measurable benefits from what you learn in these pages, but the ones who will experience the greatest transformations are those who choose to work with me (or another qualified professional) to navigate the passage together.

Both one on one and group work is so powerful, not only because others have unique perspectives that we can't access alone, but also because there is something intangible that happens when a group gathers for a shared purpose. Many people first experience this phenomenon in religious settings, where in the shared experience of worship changes take place both inside and out that are beyond words. In the Gospel of Matthew 18:20, Jesus says, "For where two or three gather in my name, there I am with them." I believe that Jesus often used the phrase "I am" to refer to the One God whom he called 'my father,' rather than to himself as a separate entity, for he did not experience the separation from Source that is the typical experience of the average person—hence his insistence that 'I and my Father are One."

In secular terms, what we observe is that at some level beyond our conscious understanding, there is something very powerful that happens when you gather with others who share your values, passions, and goals for the purpose of mutual support. This is why so-called 'Mastermind' groups have become so popular; more and more people are discovering that remarkable things happen when they gather to support each other in the process of incubating their dreams.

If you have one or two friends who share your interest in living a life of passion, purpose and joy, it might be fruitful to gather together with this book as a guide and support each other in your process of transformation. I am certain that with intention, attention, and the right attitude, this will lead to faster progress than studying the book on your own. Just be sure to keep it light and fun—this is an important ingredient for successful group work in my experience. If you do form a group and develop a greater connection with your Purpose as a result, I would love to hear about your experience.

Start With Love and Acceptance for You

If you begin to understand what you are without trying to change it, then what you are undergoes a transformation.

— Jiddu Krishnamurti

I mentioned earlier in the book that the first step on the path of transformation is acceptance, and this is absolutely true. It is also an ingredient that seems to be missing from many of the self-help books on the market today. This is understandable, since most of us are taught at a young age, whether directly or indirectly, that we are in some way not good enough. If you believe you are not good enough, then it follows that you would rather not accept where you are right now, because by definition it must not be good enough!

As you can see, this sets you up in a vicious cycle where you are continually chasing something outside of yourself to make you happy, looking for joy and success everywhere but where you are right now, and never finding it. I therefore implore you to resist the temptation to rush into the process of transformation without first acknowledging that *where you are right now has served a purpose.* If you had not made the choices that led you to where you are now, you might not find yourself ready at this juncture to make new ones that will bring you directly in line with your passion, purpose and joy. To accept yourself fully as you are right now is to release the grip of the past, freeing you to create your reality anew in the present, which is all we really ever have.

So be grateful for who you have been thus far in your life, and embrace that person completely as you prepare to take your next steps. If you are not sure how to do that, here are a few tips:

- *Examine your relationship with gratitude.* I have already spoken about gratitude earlier in the book, but there are still so many facets of this powerful practice left to explore. One of the most powerful insights I have had about gratitude over the years is that *true gratitude is unconditional.* This means that there comes a point in your evolution when you are no longer simply grateful for the people and things that you love, or when good fortune smiles upon you; rather, gratitude becomes *who you are.* Everywhere you look, you see things to be grateful for—there is no longer a need to seek them out. When gratitude becomes a way of life for you in this way, the universe will respond by bringing you more and more blessings to be grateful for. This is the Law of Attraction at work.

The trick is to not fall into the trap of being grateful from a place of lack—that is, of writing gratitude lists, etc. in the hopes that doing so will activate the Law of Attraction in your favour. There is nothing wrong with gratitude lists of course, just be aware of the state of mind from which you are writing them. If you feel a sense of expansion in your heart as you write or otherwise practice gratitude, then you know you are on the right track. If, however, you find yourself 'grasping' at what you hope to receive in the future even as you express gratitude for what you have now, this is a sign that limiting beliefs around lack in some form (either in yourself, others, or the world at large) are still dominating your vibration. Don't be discouraged if you find this to be the case; just know that spending more time on self-love may be important for you right now.

As you cultivate unconditional gratitude, you may find that you reach a place of being grateful for your past 'failures' or 'mistakes,' and even for painful experiences that have taken a long time to heal. When we truly heal and forgive, we realise that our wounds are the source of our greatest gifts, and we become free to give without any thought of reward. This is how I define a truly purposeful life, and it leads to real joy and success.

– *Ask for the gifts of the past to be revealed to you.* This is in many ways a continuation of the points I make above. What would you say if I told you that absolutely every experience in your life happened for a reason, and that if you can let enough forgiveness into your heart, you can set yourself free once and for all? If you have had traumatic experiences, you may be concerned that to fully forgive the past is to in some way condone others' harmful words and actions, but I assure you that this is not the case. Rather, forgiveness is about freeing yourself from the past, and releasing others involved to their own journeys. That said, you may be surprised at the healing that can happen in your relationships as a result of your sincere intention to forgive, even when the others involved are not aware of that intention. Underneath the things that seem to separate us we are all connected, and when we forgive, the gifts of the past are revealed to us and we are free to be our true selves at last.

– **Learn how to give to yourself that which you most wish to receive from others.** Of all the advice I share in this book, I believe this may be the most important. Why? Because when you learn to give yourself what you need, the power of others to affect your experience of life is greatly reduced. Not only that, but since we are each reflections of Source, when you give yourself what you need the Universe will echo it, often tenfold.

Of course we all need love in its many forms first, for as the Bible reminds us, 'man cannot live on bread alone.' If you know you need to feel more loved (and really, don't we all?), why wait for someone else to give you that experience? You can start by buying yourself flowers or cooking yourself your favourite meal, or you can book a massage at the end of a stressful week—do anything that makes you feel nourished and cared for, even if doing so might feel silly or self-indulgent. Act towards yourself as you would towards the person you love best, and you will be amazed at how quickly your life improves in surprising ways.

Practicing self-love is far too important to let your concerns about what others might think prevent you from giving to yourself—especially the 'others' in your own head! This is especially true when it comes to play; we all need to play, as it returns us to that state of childlike wonder and optimism that too many of us lose touch with as adults, and which puts us in a state of receptivity to all that the Universe is trying to send our way. Yet we hold back due to self-judgment, thinking 'I'm too old for that, I'll look ridiculous' and, 'what will the neighbours think if they see me doing that?' But guess what? I can tell you from my years of coaching experience that you are your own worst critic by far—in the vast majority of cases, rather than judging you for having fun, you may find that those around you are inspired by your example to make more time for fun themselves. This is a great service in this culture where we tend to take ourselves far too seriously, losing touch with our joy as a result.

If you still feel hesitant, I want you to know you have my permission to start playing *right now*! Get a trampoline for your back garden and jump on it for 15 minutes each day—it is fabulous exercise as well as being great fun. If there is something playful like that that you have always wanted to do, like learn to roller-skate or take a theatre class, I hope you will heed my advice and do it without further delay. Once you get over your initial hesitancy, there will be no going back, and you will be amazed at what it does for your overall sense of joy.

Of course, the so-called 'elephant in the room' on this topic is romantic relationships. How many people have you known who have expressed longing for a partner with very specific qualities, yet they haven't done the work to grow these qualities in themselves? In many cases such people spend years seeking their 'soul mate' in vain, and it never occurs to them to look within first.

Yet when you think about it, it makes sense, because according to the Law of Attraction like attracts like. Does this mean that you should be with someone who is exactly like you in every way? Of course not! Personally, I believe that there are a number of people who could fulfil the role of soul mate for each of us. Some of them may seem very similar to you on the surface and others may seem very different, but in either case they will find you once you heal and open your heart. There does need to be a match in values, priorities, and attitude to improve the chances that a relationship will stand the test of time, and the most sure-fire way I know to attract a match in this regard is to make sure *you are one yourself.* You need to live your life from your authenticity if you wish to attract a partner who does the same.

For this reason, I often counsel my clients who are looking for a life partner to 'become the person they wish to attract,' with spectacular results. Over and over, people are amazed to find that when they begin to treat themselves as they would wish to be treated by their beloved, a wonderful person appears seemingly out of the blue to share that experience with them. This is a very real example of how all that we need can first be found within, and when it is, the outer world will quickly change to match.

What I am getting at with all of the above points is that very often—and contrary to the thinking of many in the self-help field today—transformation is about *blossoming where you are.* If you are unhappy in your career, for example, do not assume that you can only reach your full potential by changing what you do for a living, for this is not usually the case in my experience. Rather, when you train your focus on your inner experience first, you may very well find that an opportunity soon presents itself for you to make a subtle shift in your role at work, which then allows you to more fully express your purpose.

In our doing-oriented culture it can be hard to trust this process, but I have seen it happen enough times by now to tell you with full confidence that when you love and accept yourself first—just as you are—you open the flood gates for innumerable blessings to flow your way. We are, after all, not human *doings* but human *beings*, and when we recognize this truth and act in accordance with it, we will be guided step by step from where we are to where we want to be. You are not what you do but who you choose to be, and everything you need is right here, right now—always.

Let Go of What Holds You Back For Good

I know where I'm going and I know the truth, and I don't have to be what you want me to be. I'm free to be what I want.

— Muhammad Ali

We have already discussed the power of beliefs in some detail. At this juncture, I wish to point out that the word 'belief' contains within it the word, 'lie.' This means that, no matter how much it may seem so sometimes, no belief is objectively true, and the more you practice changing your beliefs (that is, the thoughts you think over and over), the easier it will become to let them go when the time comes. Claiming your purpose and passion fully requires that you be willing to do this on an on-going basis; you must be willing to let your beliefs change with you.

Here I would like to draw your attention to a very important principle, which you can think of as the law of attraction re-stated: *what you focus on will expand in your awareness and experience.* Therefore, if a belief appears very true to you, it just means that you have been thinking it is true for a long time at a subconscious level, and are only now becoming consciously aware of it. As you work to align your beliefs with your joy, passion and purpose, remember this: if you have any ability at all to observe a limiting belief objectively, *this means that it is no longer true for you,* for we become aware of our core beliefs only when we begin to outgrow them.

If a belief is no longer true for you, then there is no need to give your energy to it any more, so why are old beliefs so hard to shake? It has been my experience that the deep, core beliefs we form as small children—the ones that are lodged in your subconscious emotional mind—are often very difficult to release without a willingness to ask for help. If you are like most people, you will experience fear to some degree as part of the process of changing your beliefs, and it is therefore very important to give yourself a safe space in which to process these emotions. You may find this space with a skilled counsellor or coach, or you may find it in a place of worship; the important thing is to call in the help you need to unwind a lifetime of unhelpful patterns. The healing you need cannot make its way to you unless you are at some level asking for it.

I have said it before and I will say it again: if anything about this process seems daunting, remember that *everything you long for resides on the other side of your fear.* What's more, it gets easier with practice—all you need to do is take the first step, and the next, and the next. Your passion, purpose and joy, and all the uncountable blessings that are headed your way, are all there waiting for you to *just say Yes*. To claim your passion and purpose right now, you have only to say Yes to the good that is already in your life, in recognition that you are a beloved child of God who is worthy of all your deepest heart's desires. It is a challenge to believe in this sometimes in today's jaded world, but when you do it becomes possible to cast aside fear and live each day to the fullest, in gratitude for each moment of your life.

CHAPTER NINE

Are You Ready?

*We must look for ways to be an active force in our own
lives. We must take charge of our own destinies, design a
life of substance and truly begin to live our dreams.*

— Les Brown in Live Your Dreams

By now there is really only one question left to ask:
are you ready to fully choose a life of purpose and
passion, or not? You have done some preliminary work to
discover and clarify what you are passionate about and how
you might bring more of your purpose into your life at a
practical level; now all that remains is to choose it. So I ask
again, *are you ready?*

Each moment of your life presents you with a myriad of
choices. Some are large, but most are so subtle that you are
not even aware of them. Living your highest and best life will
require you to pay more attention to your choices than you
have ever done in your life. As you do so, you will then be
asked to put the awareness you gain to good use making
choices that are more in alignment with your purpose.

It is a demanding proposition, and if you have a great deal of personal issues to deal with right now then it is important to acknowledge that the timing may not yet be right for you. There is a difference, however, between the recognition that you need to resolve certain issues first, and simply choosing to say 'not now' out of fear. Discernment is important here, and there is no right or wrong answer: the main thing is to always be honest with yourself.

I know that answering 'Yes' to the question "Are you ready?" requires a great deal of courage, so let me ask you some related questions:

- Do you REALLY want more joy?
- Do you REALLY want more meaning?
- Do you REALLY want more money?

If you can really choose to begin to live your purpose now, then I can tell you these things will indeed be yours. You must, however, be ready and willing to commit yourself fully to doing what it will take to become the person you were born to be, and this is no small thing.

On my own evolutionary journey, I find myself returning over and over again to the following passage from Scottish mountaineer William H. Murray, who endured three years as a prisoner of war, during the Second World War. You may have encountered it before, but I find I get a dose of determination each time I read it:

Until one is committed, there is hesitancy, the chance to draw back, always ineffectiveness. Concerning all acts of initiative (and creation), there is one elementary truth, the ignorance of which kills countless ideas and splendid plans: that the moment one definitely commits oneself, then Providence moves too. All sorts of things occur to help one that would never otherwise have occurred. A whole stream of events issues from the decision, raising in one's favour all manner of unforeseen incidents and meetings and material assistance, which no man could have dreamt would have come his way.

This passage perfectly describes another paradox that I have encountered over and over again: that it is the very act of commitment that, as Joseph Campbell observed, opens doors where before there were only walls. One definition of faith is the willingness to stay true to your vision even when obstacles arise, as they inevitably do. When you can choose to trust your inner truth no matter what life throws at you, then you know that you have what it takes to live on purpose.

Never Lose Faith

Always remember you are braver than you believe, stronger than you seem, and smarter than you think.
— Christopher Robin, to Winnie the Pooh *in The House At Pooh Corner*

I wish to point out that your Soul's reason for being here—that is, your life's purpose—may be too grand for your mind to grasp in its entirety. It may have many different facets, some of which relate to being and some to doing, and it may evolve over time as you do. Rather than attempting to grasp the whole picture, which can be overwhelming, it is important to cultivate the ability to choose to trust your inner truth moment to moment. This is faith in action.

An important companion to faith and commitment is *patience*. God's timing is always perfect, but our ego doesn't usually see it that way. To illustrate what I mean, I would like to share an allegory that often comes up in Christian circles. I encourage you to read it slowly, the better to fully take in its message. Bolded emphasis is mine. You don't need to be religious to receive its profound wisdom.

A pious man was asleep one night in his cabin when suddenly, his room filled with light and the Saviour appeared to him.

The Lord told the awed man that He had work for him to do, then led him outside and showed him a large boulder. The Lord then explained that the man was to push against the rock with all his might, for this was God's will for him.

The next morning the faithful man left early to perform this duty, and for many days he toiled from sunup to sundown, setting his shoulder squarely against the cold massive surface of the rock and pushing with all his might. Each night he returned to his cabin sore and worn out, feeling that his whole day had been spent in vain. What reason could God possibly have to ask this of him? Doubt crept into the man's heart with each day that passed, as there was no visible change in the boulder's position.

Seeing that the man showed signs of discouragement, Satan decided to enter the picture. He placed thoughts in the man's mind such as, "Why kill yourself over this? You're never going to move it!" or, "Boy, you've been at it for such a long time and you have nothing to show for it! Why don't you just give up?" Satan did his best to convince the man that the task was impossible, and furthermore **that he was an unworthy servant because he wasn't moving the massive stone.**

These doubtful thoughts discouraged and disheartened the man, until finally he started to ease up in his efforts. "Why exert myself so much?" he thought. "I'll just put forth the minimum effort, and that will be good enough." Before he could do this though, his conscience moved him to take his troubles to the Lord in prayer.

"Lord," the man said with tears in his eyes, "I have laboured so long and hard in Your service, putting forth all my strength to do what You have asked of me. Yet after all this time, I have not budged that rock even half a millimetre. What is wrong? Why am I failing?"

To the man's surprise, the Lord responded immediately. A Divine, compassionate voice said, "My friend, when long ago I asked you to serve Me, I told you to push *against that rock with all your strength, and you have done so. **But never once did I say that I expected you to move it. Your task was simply to push.** And now you come to Me, your strength spent, thinking that you have failed and ready to quit. But is this really so? Look at yourself. Your arms are strong and muscled; your back sinewy and brown. Your hands are calloused from the constant pressure, and your legs have become massive and powerful."*

*The Divine voice continued, "Through opposition you have grown much, and your ability now far surpasses that which you used to have. Yet you haven't succeeded in moving the rock, and now you come to Me with a heavy heart and your strength spent. **I, my friend, will move the rock.** Your calling was to be obedient and push, and to exercise your faith and trust in My wisdom, and this you have done. **Now, you are ready for the real work I have to give you."***

To me, there are so many nuggets of wisdom in this parable. Here are a few:

- The voice of doubt (and low self-worth) is our worst enemy
- Sometimes, you have to break down to break through
- God's timing is always perfect
- Our mission in life can bear little resemblance to what we think it "should" look like

–   Most of all: when we clarify what our true task is and dedicate ourselves to it without reservation, *the universe will take care of the rest. Always.*

There is a part of you that knows who you are and why you are here, and this voice is the voice of love, wisdom, clarity and truth. This is the voice you need to listen to, not the voice of doubt or fear. Once you find that voice within you, you need never succumb to fear again, and a life of joy and passion will be yours.

Develop A Personal Mission Statement

Writing or reviewing a mission statement changes you because it forces you to think through your priorities deeply, carefully, and to align your behaviour with your beliefs.

— Steven R. Covey, The Seven Habits of Highly-
Effective People

As you further refine your understanding of why you are here, you may find it fruitful to write out a personal mission statement. Just as organisations write mission statements to provide them with purpose and direction, you too can do the same. When done well, your personal mission statement can serve as a compass to help you better align your choices with your life's purpose.

The personal mission statement was popularised by well-known management consultant Steven R. Covey in his best-selling book *The Seven Habits of Highly-Effective People*. In the book, he describes writing your personal mission statement as "defining the personal, moral and ethical guidelines within which you can most happily express and fulfill yourself." He outlines three questions to ask yourself as you draft your personal mission statement:

- What do I want to do?
- Who do I want to help?
- What is the result? What value will I create?

The answer to the question of what you want to do should be clear by now from the work we have already done to uncover your passion and purpose. For review, below are some of the questions that I use when working with clients to clarify their life purpose. If you have already answered some of them, feel free to review your answers and add any further insights you receive this time around.

Be sure to write the first thing that pops into your head, and write without editing. Write as quickly as you are able, and preferably give yourself less than 60 seconds per question. Be honest with yourself. These are your personal and confidential notes.

1. What makes you smile? (Activities, people, events, hobbies, projects, etc.)
2. What are your favourite things to do, both in the past and in present time?
3. What activities make you lose track of time?
4. What makes you feel great about yourself?

5. Who inspires you most? (Anyone you know or do not know. It could be family, friends, authors, artists, leaders, etc.) What are the qualities within each person that inspire you? Remember, if you can see these then they exist within you as well.

6. What are you naturally good at? (Skills, talents, abilities, gifts etc.)

7. What do people typically say you are good at?

8. If you had to teach something, what would you teach?

9. What would you regret if, at the end of your life, you had not been, done or had it?

10. Imagine that you are now 100 years old, sitting in a chair in your garden; you can feel the spring breeze blowing gently against your face. You are blissful and happy, and you are pleased with the wonderful blessed life. Looking back at your life and all that you have achieved and acquired, all the relationships you have developed; what matters to you most? List them out here as fully as you can.

11. In light of your answers to the above questions, what are your deepest values?

    Now write down 9 value words in order of importance to you, with 1 being the highest and 9 the lowest priority. They can be words like family, creativity, prestige, empowerment—whatever comes to you. These words reflect your core values.

12. Draw a timeline representing the decades of your life, marking 1 as your first decade, 2 as your second decade and so on. What are some challenges, difficulties and hardships you have overcome or are in the process of overcoming? What patterns have you noticed? Where can you acknowledge yourself, or bring more forgiveness and understanding? It is so important to acknowledge the progress you have already made, for it adds much-needed fuel to your inner drive to keep growing.

13. What causes do you strongly believe in?

14. If you could get a message across to a large group of people, what would that message be?

15. Given your talents, passions and values. How might you serve, help, or contribute? (All sentient beings, causes, organisations, environment, planet, etc.)

Now that you have captured your first thoughts regarding these questions, take some time—maybe over the course of a week—to brainstorm and connect the dots between them in writing. Once you have done so, return to this place in the book to dive into the creation of your personal mission statement, which I will cover in detail next. Congratulations, for if you have gotten this far you have demonstrated the commitment required to live a life of joy, passion and purpose, and your goal is in sight!

Now you have a fresh understanding of your life's purpose, and you are ready to condense what you have learned into a statement to live by. Here are the steps that I take my clients through in the process of creating their personal mission statement:

1. Review your answers to the questions above. (You should have already done this)

2. List out words that you connect with, for example: wisdom, consciousness, empower, encourage, improve, help, give, guide, inspire, love, integrate, master, motivate, nurture, organize, produce, promote, travel, spread, share, satisfy, understand, teach, write, health, wealth, etc.

3. Based on the answers you gave earlier in the book, list everything and everyone that you believe you can help, for example people, creatures, organisations, causes, groups, environment, etc. Remember, your highest purpose is about giving first, for only then can you receive what is truly yours. In particular, write in detail about the **unique** ways in which you can serve, that no one else could quite duplicate. This is one of the clearest indications of the shape your unique life's purpose specifically takes.

5. Identify your end goal. How will the 'who' from your above answer benefit from what you 'do'?

6. Combine steps 2-4 into a few sentences. The more concise the better, but be sure to include everything that feels central to your purpose.

As you engage with this process, here are more tips to help you clarify your statement:

- Consider the legacy you would like to leave. Identify what your life roles are, and consider how you would like to be remembered for each of them. When you clarify how you want others to perceive you, it helps you step into that way of being more consciously now.

- Define SMART goals, which are Specific, Measureable, Achievable, Results-Oriented, and Time-Bound. These goals should arise out of your awareness of who inspires you and why, the legacy you wish to leave, and your purpose and aptitudes. Based on these factors, what do you want the principle outcomes of your life to be?

- As you create your goals, you may wish to create ones that are specific to each area of your life, such as relationships, career, service work, etc. The more you can identify specific actions that will move you towards each of your goals and the more manageable those goals are for you, the greater your chances of success.

- It is important to revisit both your goals and your personal mission statement at regular intervals. The frequency will be determined by the scale of the goal in question; perhaps 3 weeks for a small goal, 3 months for a medium-sized one, or 3 years for a grand one.

- Finally, while you may feel comfortable getting this far on your own, a good coach can be invaluable as you attempt to create a specific plan to address your goals. All it takes is a single session to make great progress, and doing a session quarterly or more will go a long way towards making your dreams a reality.

Once you have landed on a statement that resonates strongly for you, you may wish to print it out and place it in a special place in your home or office. Sometimes people resist writing a personal mission statement because they fear it will define them more than they would like, but this concern is unfounded. You can expect your mission statement to evolve as you do, and I recommend you revisit it periodically in order to keep it fresh and relevant to where you are now.

I trust that you will take action to develop your purpose statement. Here is my purpose statement that I would like to share with you:

My purpose is to be a Beacon of Light to release vision, creativity and intelligence. I am here to serve human kind to maximize their optimal potential and to meet and touch you at the heart and spiritual level. I am the midwife to the raising of even more consciousness. I do that through the presence of love, peace, harmony, gratitude, integrity, and learning and teaching at the highest level and in so doing change and transform my life, the lives of my clients and those with whom I make connection. I am committed to enabling you: to be your best, to be calm, centered, clear, conscious, congruent, courageous, connected, creative, caring, competent and confident.

Are You Ready For What Could Show Up In Your Life?

As you become your own advocate and your own steward, your life will beautifully transform.

— Miranda J. Barrett

Throughout this book I have driven home the point that when you really commit to living your purpose, choosing to do so even in the face of fear and uncertainty, you will be amazed at what shows up in your life as a result. There are so many stories out there of people who receive a great deal as a result of identifying and committing to their purpose. What is more, often what they receive goes far beyond anything they could have previously imagined for themselves. As I have said before, the Universe is always trying to give you your deepest heart's desire; it's just that you may not have learned how to receive it yet.

While we all love dramatic stories of miraculous co-creation and redemption, for most of us the process of living our dreams is slower and more iterative. The reason for this is simply that it *takes time* to become able to have the many blessings that the Universe is sending your way, because of the Law of Attraction. Let me explain.

There is a dissonance between the vibration that society programs you to hold, and the vibration that your soul held when you chose to incarnate with your Purpose in mind. This is not actually a problem it is just how life on Earth works. Your visions and dreams, which we have explored together, serve the purpose of propelling your growth. They point you in the direction of your soul's evolution, but you still must do the work required to get from here to there.

You may feel discouragement at this, but I assure you that it is not necessary! You have glimpsed your destiny and a flame of desire has been ignited within, but the tendency to identify with Ego causes a drop in your overall vibration that makes growth far more difficult than it needs to be. Yet when you know who you *really* are, you also know that you *will* get there in Divine timing, and the question of *when* that happens becomes irrelevant. Then you are able to simply address the step in front of you from a place of joyful presence, and this makes for a far more enjoyable journey through life!

When discussing why we are here, I always bring my clients back to the following principles:

- You are quite literally a child of God in the sense that God's essence is within you, and you therefore have full access to the glory of the Universe at all the times. It is just a matter of choosing it—simple, but not always easy! That is why it is so important not to try to walk this journey alone.

– When you know you are a Divine Being and identify with this aspect of yourself, nothing is impossible for you.

– Let the knowledge of your innate perfection silence the Ego's voices of judgment, doubt and fear, and you will experience Heaven on Earth.

You can never fully know what will show up in your life. You can only stay open to what is required of you in the Now. When you let go of your fixed ideas of the way you think that things should be, when you get out of your own way and allow life to form from the perfect organising power of nature, you flow with life. This is easy to teach, but it takes a lifetime to master. The more I learn to let go and let God, the more miracles appear in my life.

So again I ask, **are you ready for what could show up in your life when you fully embrace why you are here?** I trust you will say Yes, because **when you say Yes**, you will magically become ready, even if you did not feel so before. It is your choice to live your highest and best life that activates that potential within your field, and when you can make that choice consistently, the fun really begins!

CHAPTER TEN

The Time Is Now

The only sure thing is that if you never start, you will never arrive.

— Proverb

As we near the end of this book, you no doubt have some questions about how to proceed from here. You have deeply explored your passions and values, and this has given you a sense of your purpose. Now what you need is a clear plan of action with concrete steps to conduct you from where you are now to a life of joy, passion and purpose. Formulating such a plan is what this final chapter is about.

I have already noted that one of the easiest ways to align your life with your inner purpose is to create a list of activities that make your heart sing, and choose one to carry out each day. These activities should take no more than a half hour of your time, and they should be things that you can conceivably do on any average day. Some common examples are playing with your children or pets, playing music, going to theatre and musical concerts, walking and being with nature, creating nutritious, sumptuous meals, having tea with a cherished friend, practicing yoga or meditation, drawing or otherwise making art, or going for a run. What's important is that when you do this activity, you feel connected to your passion, optimism and wellbeing: the hallmarks of a life lived on purpose.

Action Activities to Connect With Your Purpose

I slept and dreamt that life was joy. I awoke and saw that life was service. I acted and behold, service was joy.

— Rabindranath Tagore

If you still feel unsure as to your purpose, ask yourself this: if I already knew why I am here, how would I live? There is a part of you that *does* already know your life's purpose, and its wisdom will come through if you can trick your ego into releasing its grip for a moment. There are a number of excellent techniques that I have used to capture information from beyond the conscious mind. Here are just a few:

- Meditation. If sitting meditation feels impossible (as it does for many of us in the West), an active meditation style employing visualisation may be more appropriate. Recorded meditation tracks can work wonders for getting you into a receptive state quickly.

- Stream of consciousness writing. This is best practiced after meditation, because it is important to let go of all judgment and just allow the information to flow out of you. Play with this practice periodically as a way to tune in with your higher guidance, and you will be richly rewarded.

- Let the power within you speak through your heart. Take time to relax, breathe deeply and listen to your heart. Ask your heart the questions that you are seeking answers to, then be still and listen. The answer may arrive immediately, or within hours, days or weeks. Stay tuned and become aware.

- Remember that only *you* can know your purpose. Your purpose comes from your soul; it is between you and your Creator, and it lies within your heart. You do not need to use complex psychological tools to reveal your purpose; just listen to your heart.

Once you have gained a clear sense of why you are here, you are confronted with the task of aligning your life with who you came to be. As you work to put your purpose into practice, keep the following in mind:

- **Seize every opportunity, no matter how small, to be of service.** Give naturally and without calculation or expectation of reward. Give more than you are rewarded for from a place of inner fullness, and abundance will flow your way. We must give in order to receive, and receive in order to give; many of us have issues with both, and it is in your interest to uncover and heal these within yourself, for the laws of giving and receiving are universal.

- **Remember that the Universe will support your efforts if you let it.** The Universe supports all life, and when you know that you are a part of the Universe and are therefore supported by it, that will be your reality. Problems arise only when you judge and separate yourself from the rest of Life, for this puts you in direct conflict with Reality. The fact is that you are always, already perfect, whole and provided for, and when you recognise this truth your reality will match it.

- **Give gratitude for yourself and everything in your life, each and every day.** Live with a sense of joy, and choose to view events that you consider obstacles to be perfect opportunities for you to learn and grow. If this feels difficult at times, practice forgiveness towards yourself and others, knowing that your intention to be grow in gratitude will be enough, even if it takes time.

- **Know that your goals need to *serve* your purpose, but they need *not* define your purpose.** Purpose is the engine that drives the goals you want to achieve, not the other way around.

- **Focus on solutions, rather than problems.** The mind that perceives problems can also perceive their solutions—the key is to change your perspective. If you are not seeing the solution, it is because you are not looking in the right place (or in the right way), not because it doesn't exist.

This is why working with a coach or mentor regularly is so important; their role is to help you move from your habitual, limited perspectives into new, expansive ones. From there, you will be in a position to see past the problem to the solution that has always been there, waiting to be perceived.

With the knowledge I have shared in this book and the desire to implement it, I *know* that you can live a life of greater meaning and purpose—you have only to choose and commit to it. How soon you reach your goals will simply depend upon the amount of time, energy and dedication you are able to devote to living your best life. It is perfectly natural for this to vary from person to person, and I want to emphasise that once you have chosen to walk this path, *it is counter-productive to berate yourself for not doing enough when obstacles arise.* Just resolve to always give it your best, remember the parable of the boulder, and know that your dreams will unfurl in accordance with Divine timing.

Never Give Up!

Never give in. Never give in. Never, never, never, never—in nothing, great or small, large or petty—never give in, except to convictions of honour and good sense.

— Sir Winston S. Churchill

There is no question that in the beginning the journey of following your inner truth can feel like an uphill slog, since the society we live in does not support, and in many cases directly counteracts, your intention to live on purpose. Yet despite the lack of societal support and any other life circumstance you may face, what I have observed is that it is never really an individual's circumstances that hinders them; rather, it is *their belief in their own powerlessness or lack of worth that stops their progress, every time.*

Sometimes humility is indeed called for, but too often when this is the case our ego causes us great suffering with the strength of its resistance. Yet true humility is not about submitting to another's will or feeling unworthy due to past mistakes, for in truth there are no mistakes, only opportunities for learning. When viewed through the lens of compassion and forgiveness, there is no life experience that does not offer us a lesson of some kind.

As the well-known American social researcher Brene Brown has famously observed, true humility and vulnerability are in fact emblems of great courage. When you have the courage to admit that you were wrong in perception, word, or deed, the door is opened for you to heal the wounds that keep you from living the life you were born to live. The floodgates of creation open when we let go of the need to always be right; this is why we so often need to break down in order to break through.

Of course there are always times when we feel powerless to change things that matter deeply to us, but a time inevitably comes when we must choose to exercise the one power that nothing and no one can take away: our power to choose how we respond. It is said that if you want something to change, then you must change something, and this is never more true than when it refers to our own inner attitudes.

Armed with a sense of purpose that resonates with your innermost being, you become impervious to the criticisms of others, and to doubt in any form. Take some time, ideally under the guidance of an experienced coach, to connect with why you are here on this planet. When you do, you align yourself with the flow of the Universe, and your deepest desires will manifest almost effortlessly.

Let Purpose Drive Your Life

What you get by achieving your goals is not as important as what you become by achieving your goals.

— Henry David Thoreau

Living your purpose is, without question, the greatest feeling in the world. It is like reaching the summit of your own personal Mount Everest, where you have a clear sense of who you are and where your destiny lies each and every moment. When you are letting your purpose drive your life, you exude self-confidence, self-reliance and self-assurance, which in turn inspire the confidence of those around you.

What's more, you feel a sense of personal power, strongly centred and rooted in your Being, which enables you to be emotionally resilient. You are focused on your intentions and accomplishments, and you radiate peace and happiness. You are content with your choices, even in the face of adversity or ambiguity. You remain positive, optimistic and in alignment with your desired outcome, knowing that energy flows to wherever you place your attention.

Living your purpose activates your success blueprints at an energetic level, causing people, things and circumstances that can help you accomplish your goals to naturally flow to you. You recognise that you are in the right place at the right time and with the right people, more and more of the time. Prosperity flows to you because you have removed the negative thoughts and limiting beliefs that were creating resistance in your vibrational field, allowing what you have been seeking to find you.

Can you feel how, from this place, anything is possible? Let me assure you that there is nothing more powerful that you can do than living your purpose for your work, your relationships, and every other aspect of your life. When you put your purpose in the driver's seat, magic happens—there is no better way to say it than that!

The whole Universe is sending you messages and guidance on your purpose, so listen to your inner drum and allow yourself to live your purpose. When you do so you become more attractive with more vitality, you live a more meaningful life, and you will find yourself at the right place, at the right time with the right people. Your soul stays in constant communication with you, and your soul's greatest desire is for you to fulfil your purpose for your life.

Knowing your purpose and passion is the first step to living a meaningful life. It is through living with purpose that you achieve your greatest potential. The tragedy is that most people have never taken the time to think nor reflect on their purpose. The pain of not being aware of your purpose means that you may go through life not recognising that you have a choice. You could be quite disconnected and living a life of quiet desperation and not knowing why your life is not within the flow and desire of your heart.

I say to you now:

You need something to believe in, something for which you can have whole-hearted enthusiasm. You need to feel that your life has meaning, that you are needed in this world.

Perhaps best of all, identifying your purpose for being on the planet takes the guesswork out of making important life decisions. As you combine what you love to do with what you want to accomplish in the world, you begin to comprehend what you are supposed to be doing with your life. In this way, discovering your purpose can save you a lot of frustration, money, headaches, heartaches and time.

When you are fully engaged with work you enjoy and at your very best, you are happy. In this state you feel joyful and purposeful. You will sleep with comfort and everything in your life falls into place to make life worthwhile. When you feel this way it becomes easier for you to stay open to what is happening in your life and adjust to changing situations and circumstances. This, in turn, makes following the path of your destiny much less difficult. You now have the inner fortitude to face challenges with clarity and strength of purpose, ensuring your triumph.

So what I want to know is, will you join me on this journey? Will you give yourself to your purpose now, fully and without reservation? Remember that your purpose helps you come fully alive, and what the world needs more than anything else right now is people who have come alive. There is no greater service you can offer than to be who your heart knows you are meant to be, and serve from that place.

If you like, you can think of this journey as a pilgrimage undertaken for the sake of your true Self—the one that knows you are Divine and limitless in your potential. Like a pilgrim walking to a holy shrine, it is your faith that will conduct you safely to your destination, providing you with exactly what you need, when you need it. You have only to stay connected to your longing for that which calls you to stay on the path, no matter how many twists and turns it may take.

The time and place is now, and I look forward to meeting you on the road soon, as a fellow traveller.
I would love to hear from you.

Please join my Facebook Group:
https://www.facebook.com/NeslynWatsonDruee/

Email me at:
Neslyn@Neslyn.com

CHAPTER ELEVEN

Conclusion: Today is the First Day of the Rest of Your Life

Throughout these pages I have been with you as a consciousness coach, to enable you to reach the realm of your greatness, to show you the map and help you navigate the territory that will inspire you and give you signposts to lead your life, your business and your enterprise with courage, authenticity, love, wisdom and grace from the Divine Light of Spirit.

As we wrap up our time together, I want you to commit the following statement to your memory:

It's not about the life you are living; it's about creating a life you want to have lived.

Earlier in these pages, I defined success as you living your purpose and me living mine. My purpose is to lead you to the realm of your greatness and to empower you to become more conscious—healthy, wealthy, wise and free—and to enable you to become aware of your abilities and inspired to lead with courage, authenticity, love, and wisdom.

Now you know that you are living your soul's purpose when:

- You feel joyful;
- You are in awe of the wonder of life around you, and
- You are being of service to others, and when you are deeply aware of your connection with God.

You also know that as a result of living your purpose:

- Your life can be magical
- You will pursue your goals simply because they are so exciting
- You *can* achieve your dreams
- You can do what you love and have an abundant life
- You can have happy and fulfilling relationships

In other words, when you are able to combine your purpose and your passion to make profits, you find the Holy Grail—you hit the jackpot!

When you work with me you will go through the ultimate life success formula, and this is the result you will create: doing what you love.

In the orchestra of life, you have a unique role to play that no one else can fulfil. Each of us has a contribution to offer the world that only we can make: what is yours?

I believe that when you are living your purpose in truth and sincerity, you are living your soul's desire and carrying out the mission you incarnated to fulfil. In coaching you to help you find your purpose and live an extraordinary life, I will teach you how to communicate with yourself so that you develop the confidence required to obtain positive outcomes. You will leave with valuable frameworks and blueprints for living your joy.

People who are coached by me report that after one session they gain clarity, insight, a sense of purpose and more focused energy. They have a different perspective on how their life could be, and they become even more connected with their creator. They know what they are going to do to make their choice certain and actual in the near future.

I leave you with the invitation to commit to coaching to move you to the realm of your greatness, to empower you to become conscious of your purpose, to inspire you to lead your life with courage, authenticity, love, and wisdom through the Divine light of Spirit. Join the membership of Neslyn.com now to learn how to empower yourself even more at: http://neslyn.com

If you are ready to access breakthrough coaching and move to the next step in your life, then do so by taking action at: http://neslyn.com/coaching/

You may also engage with me by requesting a complementary coaching strategy to assess if we are able to work together by completing a coaching strategy questionnaire. You may access this questionnaire at: http://neslyn.com/coaching-strategy/

Who do you know who might benefit from my webinars, seminars and workshops? I encourage you to share the link to my website with them that they may realise their own purpose, calling and fulfilment in their lives.

I look forward to connecting with you.

— Dr Neslyn Watson-Druée, CBE

39223941R00094

Printed in Poland
by Amazon Fulfillment
Poland Sp. z o.o., Wrocław